A FEW GOOD MEN

by

AARON SORKIN

SAMUEL FRENCH, INC.

45 West 25th Street   NEW YORK 10010

7623 Sunset Boulevard HOLLYWOOD 90046

LONDON   TORONTO

IMPORTANT BILLING AND CREDIT REQUIREMENTS

A Few Good Men was originally presented at the Heritage Repertory Theatre of the University of Virginia, Department of Drama, and subsequently, in association with the John F. Kennedy Center for the Performing Arts, was presented at the Music Box Theatre in New York, on November 15, 1989, under the direction of Don Scardino, with Dianne Trulock as production stage manager, and with designs by: Ben Edwards, set; David C. Woolard, costume; Thomas R. Skelton, light; and John Gromada, sound; and with the following cast:

SENTRY	Ron Ostrow
Lance Cpl. HAROLD W. DAWSON	Victor Love
Pfc LOUDEN DOWNEY	Michael Dolan
Lt. j.g. SAM WEINBERG	Mark Nelson
Lt. j.g. DANIEL A KAFFEE	Tom Hulce
Lt. Cmdr. JOANNE GALLOWAY	Megan Gallagher
Capt. ISAAC WHITAKER	Edmond Genest
Capt. MATTHEW A. MARKINSON	Robert Hogan
Pfc. WILLIAM T. SANTIAGO	Arnold Molina
Lt. Col. NATHAN JESSEP	Stephen Lang
Lt. JONATHAN JAMES KENDRICK	Ted Marcoux
Lt. JACK ROSS	Clark Gregg
Cpl. JEFFREY OWEN HOWARD	Geoffrey Nauffts
Capt. JULIUS ALEXANDER RANDOLPH	Paul Butler
Cmdr. WALTER STONE	Fritz Sperberg

MARINES, SAILORS, M.P.'s, LAWYERS, et al.

Stephen Bradbury, Jeffrey Dreisbach, Michael Genet, George Gerdes, Joshua Malina

Timothy Busfield replaced Tom Hulce on May 14, 1990.

CHARACTERS

Sentry
Pfc. Louden Downey
Lt. j.g. Sam Weinberg
Lt. j.g. Daniel A. Kaffee
Lt. Cmdr. Joanne Galloway
Capt. Isaac Whitaker
Capt. Matthew A. Markinson
Pfc. William T. Santiago
Lt. Col. Nathan Jessep
Lt. Jonathan James Kendrick
Lt. Jack Ross
Cpl. Jeffrey Owen Howard
Capt. Julius Alexander Randolph
Cmdr. Walter Stone
Marines, Sailors, M.P.'s, Lawyers, et al.

SCENE

The action takes place in various locations in Washington, D.C., and on the United States Naval Base in Guantanamo Bay, Cuba.

TIME

Summer, 1986

SCENE: The stage is slightly raked and made up of wooden planks. Upstage and slightly right of Center is a Marine Sentry Tower, in front of which, running the width of the stage, is a barbed-wire fence. The only other set pieces are plain wooden tables and chairs which will be moved throughout the play by the actors. All settings of the play will be created by light, sound, clothing and text. For the Broadway production, Ben Edward's set had three levels. In this script, the Downstage level is referred to as #1, the middle level #2, and the top level #3. Scenes will frequently overlap, with the end of one scene bleeding into the beginning of the next.

AT RISE: LIGHTS up on Dawson and Downey. with two MP's standing behind them.

DAWSON. I, Lance Corporal Harold W. Dawson, have been informed by Special Agent R.C. McGuire of the Naval Investigative Service, that I am suspected of Conspiracy to Commit Murder, Murder, and Conduct Unbecoming a United States Marine, in the matter of Private William T. Santiago. I have also been advised that I have the right to remain silent and make no statement at all.

DOWNEY. Any statement I do make can be used against me in a trial by court -martial or other judicial or administrative proceeding. I have the right to consult with a lawyer prior to further questioning.

DAWSON. I am presently assigned to Rifle Security Company Windward, Second Platoon Delta, NAVBASE, Guantanamo Bay, Cuba.

DOWNEY. I am a Pfc. in the United States Marine Corps, assigned to Marine Rifle Security Company, Windward, Second Platoon Delta. I will have been in the Marine Corps ten months as of August.

DAWSON. I entered Private Santiago's barracks room on the evening of 7 July, at or about 23:50. I was accompanied by Pfc. Louden Downey.

DOWNEY. I was accompanied by my Squad Leader, Lance Corporal Harold W. Dawson.

DAWSON. We tied his hands and feet with rope.

DOWNEY. We tied Private Santiago's hands and feet with rope and we forced a piece of cloth into his mouth.

DAWSON. We placed duct tape over his eyes and mouth.

DOWNEY. I have read this two page statement that Special Agent McGuire has prepared for me at my request, as we discussed its content. I have been allowed to make all changes and corrections, initializing those changes and corrections.

DAWSON. These statements are true and factual to the best of my knowledge.

(*LIGHTS change to Kaffee's office as SAM enters. KAFFEE's in a hurry.*)

SAM. Danny, you know what I just saw?

KAFFEE. Sam, I'm late.

SAM. There's a lady from Captain Bronsky's office walking around the halls.

KAFFEE. Is she stealing things?

SAM. No.

KAFFEE. What's the problem?

SAM. Danny, ordinarily when the Office of the Judge Advocate General sends a lawyer around to talk to the lawyers, it means someone's screwed up.

KAFFEE. Have you done anything wrong?

SAM. No.

KAFFEE. You sure?

SAM. Yeah. I think so. I don't know. I've been tired lately. Look, do me a favor, would you?

KAFFEE. (*Puts three folders into his case, and picks up a Yoo-Hoo.*) Sure.

SAM. If she mentions anything about DeMattis, you know, the engineer, my guy who was littering in the Admiral's tulip garden, would you cover me?

KAFFEE. Sure.

SAM. Yeah?

KAFFEE. (*Crosses R to steps and up onto 2nd level.*) I don't know what you're talking about, but sure, no problem.

SAM. (*Follows to top step.*) Danny—

KAFFEE. Sam, I'm late for a plea bargain. I'm representing an Ensign who bought and smoked ten dollars worth of oregano.

SAM. He thought it was dope?

KAFFEE. What's his defense?

SAM. His defense? His defense is I'm a schmuck.

KAFFEE. Actually, I smoked some of the stuff, it wasn't that bad.

SAM. You're not concerned?

KAFFEE. Oh, please, what's he gonna be charged with, possession of a condiment?

SAM. Danny, I'm talking about the lady from T-JAG.

KAFFEE. Sam, my softball team's playing Bethesda Medical tomorrow. I can't be concerned with anything right now. I'll see you at lunch. (*HE exits LC #2; SAM exits RC #2.*)

(*LIGHTS up on Whitaker's office.*)

JO. I'm Lt. Commander Joanne Galloway, sir.

WHITAKER. Isaac Whitaker, come on in.

JO. Thank you, Captain. I appreciate your seeing me on such short notice.

WHITAKER. Bronsky said it was important. Something about re-opening a case.

JO. Yes sir.

WHITAKER. Bronsky's an old friend.

JO. He speaks very highly of you, sir.

WHITAKER. Crapolla.

JO. (*Sits, putting her attaché SL of her chair.*) Yes sir.

WHITAKER. I've seen you around here, haven't I? You work across the yard at Appellate.

JO. My desk is at Appellate, but actually I work directly for the Office of the Judge Advocate General as a Special Investigator in Internal Affairs.

WHITAKER. Of course, now I know how I know you. Your footprint has been tattooed to my behind any number of times.

JO. I don't know that I'd put it quite that way.

WHITAKER. You were the one who recycled those fourteen B misdemeanors last winter.

JO. Yes, I believe that was me.

WHITAKER. Fourteen B misdemeanors. Drunk and Disorderly, we had 'em closed.

JO. The blue copies of the charge sheet weren't filed to Division with the IC-1.

WHITAKER. Who gives a damn?

JO. There are rules, sir. I'm sure you understand.

WHITAKER. You had these guys working Christmas day, writing out charge sheets in long hand. Christmas day, Commander.

JO. It was in the interest of justice, sir.

WHITAKER. Can I ask you a question?

JO. Of course, Captain.

WHITAKER. Are you here to bust anyone's ass?

JO. Absolutely not, sir. No. Not at all. Only if necessary.

WHITAKER. Fine then. (*Sits.*) What can I do for you?

JO. I'd like to request a favor.

WHITAKER. Good luck.

(*During the following, an MP enters RC #2 with DAWSON and DOWNEY. THEY sit on the DS side of ramp leading to top level #3.*)

JO. (*Stands, handing folder to Whitaker.*) Two prisoners are being held in Guantanamo Bay, Cuba. They pleaded to Murder 2, Conspiracy to Commit and Conduct Unbecoming.

(*MP exits RC #2.*)

JO. I petitioned JAG to deny the guilty pleas.

WHITAKER. What's the problem, did someone misspell conspiracy?

JO. No sir. They confessed to murder at three in the morning at a nineteen-minute hearing without counsel. It's my sense that there's much more to this than what's written in the Division report. Which brings me to my request.

WHITAKER. (*Looks over the material in the folder.*) Yes?

JO. It's not a request so much as a recommendation.

WHITAKER. Yes?

JO. I think the attorney assigned to the case should have a certain energy. A real go-getter. Someone who possesses not only the legal skill, but a familiarity with the inner workings of the military and a singular passion for justice.

In short, Captain, if I may be so bold, I'd like to suggest myself.

WHITAKER. Imagine my surprise.

JO. (*Sits, takes out Bronsky's letter of recommendation from side section of attaché and turns to Whitaker.*) I've brought a letter of recommendation from Captain Bronsky. (*Hands him the letter, which HE does not open.*)

WHITAKER. You work for T-JAG, you're a special investigator, why do you want to get mixed up in grunt work again?

JO. I don't consider it grunt work, sir.

WHITAKER. It's gonna be a ten-minute plea bargain and a week of paper work.

JO. I would look forward to it with relish, sir.

WHITAKER. Do you always talk like this?

JO. I'm anxious to make a good impression.

WHITAKER. Relax.

JO. Yes, sir.

WHITAKER. So you want to take on trial work again?

JO. On, with a vengeance, sir.

WHITAKER. How many cases did you handle when you were with the department?

JO. Altogether?

WHITAKER. Yes.

JO. Six.

WHITAKER. How'd you do?

JO. From what perspective?

WHITAKER. Your client's.

JO. Not well.

WHITAKER. Ah.

(*DAVE, a lawyer, enters DL with an open inter-office envelope and crosses UR of Jo to Whitaker.*)

JO. Those cases were lost on their merits, sir.

DAVE. I'm sorry, Isaac. This just came for you.

WHITAKER. Thank you. This is Lt. Commander Galloway.

DAVE. Really?

JO. How do you do.

DAVE. (*Shakes hands with Jo.*) Really enjoyed last Christmas.

WHITAKER. That'll be all.

(*DAVE exits DL. WHITAKER removes several pages from the envelope and looks them over.*)

JO. (*Standing.*) So what do you say?

WHITAKER. (*Standing.*) Commander, may I call you Joanne?

JO. Yes, please, Jo.

WHITAKER. Jo, you seem like a fairly harmless neurotic person—

JO. I appreciate that.

WHITAKER. And I'd like to help you out, but there are two things preventing me. The first is that despite your excellent credentials, it would appear that as a litigator, you suck.

JO. Yes, but I'm sure—

WHITAKER. The second is that JAG already detailed a lawyer.

JO. (*This stops her.*) They did?

WHITAKER. (*Shows her the contents of the envelope.*) You must've convinced 'em this was pretty important. JAG never cares who I assign in this district.

JO. Well ... all right. (*Turns and picks up attaché.*)

WHITAKER. Tough break. (*Hands back letter and folder.*) It was nice talking to you, I'll see you around.

JO. (*Turns, starts to exit DL; stops, and turns to him.*) Captain—

WHITAKER. Isaac.

JO. Isaac, would you mind if I met with the attorney, just for a few minutes.

WHITAKER. We have a staff meeting at three, I'll be giving out assignments then.

JO. Excellent. Thank you.

WHITAKER. Try not to make anybody nervous.

JO. Yes, sir.

WHITAKER. I'll see you then. Conference Room 4.

JO. Thank you, Isaac. (*Remembering*.) Oh, Isaac?

WHITAKER. Jo?

JO. What's the name of the attorney?

WHITAKER. Daniel Kaffee.

(*JO exits DL; WHITAKER remains seated.*
LIGHTS up on the brig.
DAWSON and DOWNEY continue to sit in silence.
    FOOTSTEPS are heard coming from UR #3.)

DAWSON. Ten hut. Officer on deck.

(*DAWSON and DOWNEY stand at attention as*
    MARKINSON enters UR #3 and walks up to the cell.)

MARKINSON. (*Quietly and with difficulty*.) They're giving you a lawyer. They're gonna move you up to Washington, D.C. and give you a lawyer who's gonna ask you some questions. I want you to remember something about these lawyers. They don't care about anything. The don't care about honor. Or loyalty. They don't care about the United States Marine Corps. They don't even care about you. They're clowns. That's why, so help me God, they're the only ones who can save you right now. I want you boys to be smart. Talk to the lawyer.

WHITAKER. I'd just settle for the O.T.H. It's his fourth U.A. You're not gonna do any better than that.

MARKINSON. That's all. (*HE exits.*)

(*LIGHTS up on a staff meeting.*)

LYLE. What about a motion to suppress?

WHITAKER. On what grounds?

LYLE. Grounds?

DAVE. See, this is where your strategy begins to fall apart.

WHITAKER. Take the O.T.H.

(*KAFFEE enters DL.*)

KAFFEE. Excuse me. Sorry I'm late.

WHITAKER. Well, I'm sure you have a good excuse.

KAFFEE. No, ... I just didn't really care enough about this meeting to be on time.

DAWSON. At ease.

WHITAKER. He's kidding. Commander Galloway, this is Lt. Kaffee.

KAFFEE. How do you do.

JO. You're a j.g.

KAFFEE. I beg your pardon?

JO. (*To Whittaker.*) I wrote a 17 page memo petitioning Division, they assigned a junior grade?

WHITAKER. Yeah.

KAFFEE. Did I miss something?

WHITAKER. Commander Galloway's from T-JAG.

KAFFEE. Oh, ahh ... Whatever Sam did, it wasn't his fault. He's been tired. (*To Sam.*) How's that?

SAM. Thanks so much.

KAFFEE. Sam's pretty sure his little girl's about to say her first word any day now.

WHITAKER. Really? I didn't know that.

SAM. She just looks like she has something to say.

WHITAKER. She's 14 months old, what does she have to say?

KAFFEE. We've got a little pool going in the office. Ten bucks. Pick a word off the grid.

WHITAKER. What's left?

KAFFEE. "Rosebud."

WHITAKER. I'll pass. Kaffee, this is yours. (*Passes out some folders.*) You've been detailed by JAG.

KAFFEE. Detailed to do what?

WHITAKER. Detailed to handle this.

WHITAKER. Everybody listen up. Guantanamo Bay, Cuba. A Pfc. named William Santiago (*SANTIAGO sits on the LC platform step writing.*) writes a letter to his Senator claiming that he knows the name of a Marine on the base who illegally fired a round from his weapon over the fenceline. Santiago ends the letter by saying he wants a transfer off the base in exchange for the identity of the felon.

KAFFEE. What's a fenceline?

WHITAKER. Sam?

SAM. A big wall separating the good guys from the bad guys.

KAFFEE. Teacher's pet.

WHITAKER. Gentlemen.

KAFFEE. Santiago writes a letter saying he'll reveal some guy's name. Do we know who?

WHITAKER. Lance Corporal Harold Dawson, his squad leader—

KAFFEE. Uh-oh.

WHITAKER. Dawson, by the way, claims that it wasn't an illegal shooting, that he was engaged at his post by a Cuban sentry, and was returning fire. The fenceline shooting, however, is absolutely beside the point.

KAFFEE. What's the point?

WHITAKER. Santiago's dead.

SAM. What happened?

WHITAKER. Dawson and another member of his squad, a Pfc. Louden Downey, (*Crosses UR of Jo.*) break into Santiago's room, tie him up, and stick a rag down his throat. You can see on page five, the attending physician says the rag was treated with some kind of toxin.

KAFFEE. They poisoned the rag?

WHITAKER. Not according to them.

KAFFEE. What do they say?

WHITAKER. Not much. Commander Galloway looked at their statements and had them recycled. They'll be brought up here to Washington in the morning and on Thursday at Oh-six-hundred, you'll catch a transport down to Cuba for the day to see what you can see.

WHITAKER. You'll report to the barracks CO, Lt. Colonel Nathan Jessep, you know anything about him?

KAFFEE. Should I?

JO. Golden Boy of the Corps,

JO. He's the youngest Colonel in the North American command. He's got his eyes set on the National Security Council.

WHITAKER. Thank you, Commander. If Jessep's got anything good to say about the defendants, it'll help. Any questions?

KAFFEE. Was that Oh-six-hundred in the morning, sir?

JO. Excuse me.

WHITAKER. Yes?

JO. Lt. Kaffe, have you ever been in a courtroom?

WHITAKER. Commander—

JO. Jo.

WHITAKER. Jo, if this goes to court, they won't need a lawyer, they'll need a priest.

JO. No, they'll need a lawyer.

KAFFEE. Isaac, I want to say for the record that this is the least fun I've ever had at one of your staff meetings.

JO. Captain, there are two defendants. JAG only assigned them one attorney?

WHITAKER. Yeah, well, there are sworn confessions. I'm sure Kaffee can handle the plea bargain himself. He's closed 39 cases in six months.

KAFFEE. One more and I get a set of steak knives.

JO. It just seems to me that six months down the line, Appellate's gonna look at this and open it up again on the grounds of insufficient representation.

(*An uncomfortable silence.*)

KAFFEE. No offense taken, if you were wondering.

JO. Having one attorney represent both defendants might look strange to an unusually thorough investigator.

WHITAKER. This is JAG's assignment, not mine, I don't—

JO. Actually, you have the authority to appoint co-counsel.

WHITAKER. Jo, it's an open and shut—

JO. I think Christmas is a time when people should be with their loved ones, don't you, Captain?

WHITAKER. Sam.

SAM. Me?

WHITAKER. Work with Kaffee on this.

SAM. Doing what?

WHITAKER. Various administrative ... You know ... Things. Sit second chair.

SAM. In other words, I have no responsibilities whatsoever.

WHITAKER. Right.

SAM. My kinda case.

WHITAKER. The two of you, listen to me, this is important. You've got some leverage on this, but not much.

KAFFEE. What kinda leverage?

WHITAKER. This letter that Santiago wrote wasn't the first.

JO. In fact, it was the twelfth. He put in for transfer six times in eight months, nobody was listening. This last letter was just a last ditch effort.

WHITAKER. Thank you, Commander.

JO. Jo.

KAFFEE. Do we have the letters?

WHITAKER & JO. Yeah.

KAFFEE. Am I right in assuming they don't paint a flattering picture of Marine Corps life in Guantanamo Bay?

WHITAKER. That's right.

KAFFEE. Am I also right in assuming that if the letters, as well as the assault, were kept as quiet as possible, that the Government might feel pre-disposed to offer a degree of leniency to the defendants?

WHITAKER. Right again.

KAFFEE. Steak knife city.

WHITAKER. All right, look, don't get cute down there. The Marines in Guantanamo are fanatical.

KAFFEE. About what?

(*LIGHTS up on SANTIAGO.*)

SANTIAGO. Dear Senator ...

WHITAKER. About being Marines. Moving on ...

SANTIAGO. My name is Pfc. William T. Santiago. I am a Marine stationed at Marine Barracks, Windward, Guantanamo Bay, Cuba. I am writing to inform you of my problems and to ask for your help. Wednesday, May 18th, we were out on a PT run. I've fallen out on runs before for several reasons, such as feeling dizzy or nauseated, and on the 18th, we were running and I'd fallen back about 20 or 30 feet going down a rocky, unstable hill. My sergeant deliberately grabbed me and pushed me down the hill. Then I saw all black and the last thing I remember is hitting the deck. I was brought to the hospital where I was told I just had heat exhaustion and was explained to by the doctor that my body had trouble with the hot sun and I hyperventilate. I was put in remedial physical training and punished by filling sandbags every day after I stand my post on the fenceline. I ask you to help me. Please, sir, I just need to be transferred out of RSC.

(*LIGHTS up on Jessep's office as TOM enters.*)

TOM. Excuse me, sir, Captain Markinson and Lt. Kendrick to see you.
JESSEP. Thank you, Tom.

(*MARKINSON and KENDRICK enter.*)

MARKINSON. Good morning, Colonel.
JESSEP. Matthew, Jon, have a set.
MARKINSON. Thank you, sir. (*HE sits.*)
JESSEP. Gumball?
MARKINSON. No. Thanks.
JESSEP. Jon? Gumball?
KENDRICK. Thank you, no sir.
JESSEP. Ten-hundred hours, it's already hot enough out there to melt the brass right off your collar. I just had a Navy guy in here telling me that we were lucky, after all it's "dry heat." Dry heat? It's a hundred and seven degrees outside, how am I supposed to feel about that? Matthew, you've been here the longest, is this about as hot as it gets or am I actually trapped in hell?

MARKINSON. This is about the hottest it's been since maybe '84, Colonel.

JESSEP. Is that right?

MARKINSON. I believe so.

JESSEP. '84 was pretty bad was it?

MARKINSON. Got up to a hundred and nineteen.

JESSEP. "Capering half in smoke and half in fire." (*Pause.*) Moby Dick. (*Pause.*) Jon, when I quote Melville, you don't have to nod your head up and down like you know what I'm talking about.

KENDRICK. Yes, sir.

JESSEP. I'm not gonna regard you as less of a man because you're not well read.

KENDRICK. Thank you, sir.

JESSEP. I mean that.

KENDRICK. I appreciate that, sir.

JESSEP. Sure you won't have a gumball?

KENDRICK. Thank you, sir.

JESSEP. (*To Markinson.*) 119 Fahrenheit.

MARKINSON. Yes sir.

JESSEP. I'll bet you had Marines passing out right and left.

MARKINSON. Actually no. The men were all right.

JESSEP. Nobody passed out? Or got dizzy? No dehydration?

MARKINSON. Not that I recall.

JESSEP. Impressive.

MARKINSON. Yes sir.

JESSEP. (*To Kendrick.*) You know why those Marines didn't pass out in '84, Jonathan? Even though it was 119 degrees by Captain Markinson's reckoning? You know why they stayed on the job?

KAFFEE. Why, sir?

JESSEP. 'Cause that's what they're fuckin' trained to do.

KENDRICK. Yes, sir.
JESSEP. Who the fuck is Pfc. William T. Santiago?!

(*LIGHTS up on brig.*)

MP. Ten-hut.
JO. Good morning, my name's Joanne Galloway.
DAWSON. Ma'am. Lance Corporal Harold W. Dawson, ma'am. Marine Barracks, Rifle Security Company Windward.
DOWNEY. Ma'am. Private First Class Louden Downey, ma'am.
JO. Stand at ease. I work for the Navy JAG Corps. I'm the one who had you guys brought up here. I just wanted to stop in and see if there was anything you needed. (*Pause.*) Or any questions you wanted to ask. (*Pause.*) I'm sure you're both pretty confused and frightened ... and so anything I can help you with ... any questions you might have ...
DOWNEY. Ma'am, permission to speak?
JO. Go ahead.
DOWNEY. I got some Spiderman's and some Batman's sittin' in my footlocker. Somebody'll dog 'em for sure if they're not secured, ma'am.
JO. You think this is a joke?
DOWNEY. Ma'am, no ma'am!
JO. How 'bout you, Corporal, is this a joke?
DAWSON. No ma'am, it's not a joke, ma'am!
DOWNEY. I apologize to the Commander, ma'am. I certainly didn't mean nothin'. About the books, ma'am. I didn't mean nothin'.
JO. (*Pause.*) You were read your Article 31 rights, did you understand them?
DAWSON. Yes, ma'am.
JO. (*To Downey.*) Did you understand them?

DOWNEY. Yes, ma'am.

JO. Say you understand them.

DOWNEY. Ma'am. I understand them, ma'am.

JO. (*Thinks for a moment, then calls out:*) Can I get an MP. (*To Dawson.*) Corporal, I'm gonna talk to Private Downey alone for a minute.

(*MP enters.*)

DAWSON. Yes, ma'am.

JO. Would you take Corporal Dawson into a holding room, please.

MP. Aye, aye, Commander.

(*DAWSON doesn't move.*)

MP. Let's go.

(*HE still doesn't move.*)

MP. Hey!

DAWSON. Ma'am? Permission to be dismissed.

JO. You're dismissed.

(*DAWSON turns and exits followed by the MP.*)

JO. Hi. (*Opens folder.*) Your only living relative over the age of 18 is Ginny Miller, your aunt on your mother's side, is that correct?

(*DOWNEY doesn't respond. He's scared as hell.*)

JO. Ginny Miller?

DOWNEY. Yes, ma'am.

JO. She hasn't been contacted yet, would you like me to contact her? (*Pause.*) I'll take care of that for you. (*Pause.*) Private, do you know why you're here? (*Pause. — Downey's not real good at pop quizzes.*)

DOWNEY. Ma'am, this is where the guard told me to stand.

(*Pause.*)

JO. Louden? May I call you Louden?
DOWNEY. Yes, ma'am.
JO. Do you know where you are?

(*A silence long enough for Jo to determine that Downey hasn't a clue.*)

JO. Do you know why you've been arrested?
DOWNEY. Willy died, ma'am.
JO. (*Pause.*) Why? (*Forget it, there's no way he knows the answer to this one.*) Was it an accident, or did you mean to do it?
DOWNEY. Ma'am?
JO. Why did you want to hurt Santiago?
DOWNEY. (*Twelve hours a day on the Cuban fenceline is easy, answering questions without Dawson in the room is hard.*) It was a Code Red, ma'am.
JO. What's a Code Red? (*That might have been a mistake.*) Louden?
DOWNEY. Ma'am. I don't need those comic books. You can have 'em if you like, ma'am.
JO. What's a Code Red?
DOWNEY. (*What did Markinson say ...*) Ma'am, permission to speak?
JO. Sure.

DOWNEY. Are ... Are you ... are you my lawyer, ma'am?

(*Pause.*)

JO. I'm —no. I'm a lawyer, but I'm not—I won't be representing you.

DOWNEY. Ma'am, Captain Markinson told us to talk to our lawyer, ma'am. That's what he told us to do.

(*LIGHTS up on softball field.*)

KAFFEE. (*Calls out to unseen players.*) All right, man on first, one down, let's go for two! (*To someone a little closer.*) Hit a few out to Sherby. (*Out to the field.*) Get your glove down, Sherby, you gotta get your glove down. Pick up some dirt with that ball.

(*JO crosses toward Kaffee.*)

KAFFEE. Let's do it again. Man on first, one down, let's go for two!

JO. Excuse me—

KAFFEE. (*Turns to see her.*) One second. (*Out to the field.*) I need you to trust me, Sherby. If you keep your eyes open while the ball is coming toward you, your chances of catching the ball increase by a factor of ten (*To Jo.*) You want to suit up? We need all the help we can get.

JO. No, thank you. I can't throw and catch things.

KAFFEE. (*Crosses DRC.*) That's too bad, cause—

JO. I wanted to talk to you about Corporal Dawson and Pfc. Downey.

KAFFEE. Those names sound like they should mean something to me, but it's just not clicking in.

JO. Harold Dawson and Louden Downey.

KAFFEE. (*Pause.*) If you could just give me one more hint, I could—

JO. Dawson! Downey! Your clients!

KAFFEE. The Cuba thing! Yes! Dawson and Downey. (*Pause. Crosses to Jo.*) Right. I was—I don't know, for a second—but, yes. (*Pause.*) Lance Corporal Dawson and ...

JO. ... Pfc. Downey.

KAFFEE. Yes. (*Pause.*) I'm sorry. I've forgotten your name.

JO. Lt. Commander Joanne Galloway.

KAFFEE. (*Pause.*) I've done something wrong, haven't I?

JO. Yes. I was wondering why two guys have been in jail since this morning while their lawyer is outside hitting a ball.

KAFFEE. We need the practice.

JO. That wasn't funny.

KAFFEE. It was a little funny.

JO. Have you read the IC-1?

KAFFEE. You mean, like ... actually read it?

JO. No, I mean have you read it in the abstract.

KAFFEE. No, it's on my desk. Very close to the top of the pile.

JO. Lieutenant, would you feel very insulted if I recommended to your supervisor that he assign different counsel?

KAFFEE. Why?

JO. I'm not sure how to say this without possibly hurting your feelings, but I don't think you're fit to handle this defense.

KAFFEE. You don't even know me. Normally it takes someone hours to discover I'm not fit to handle a defense. Oh come on, that was damn funny.

JO. (*Almost confidential.*) I do know you. I know you went to Harvard Law on a Navy scholarship and I know that you're probably just treading water for the three years you've gotta serve, just kinda laying low till you can get out and get a real job, and that's fine and I won't tell anyone. But my feeling is that if this case is handled in the same fast food slick-ass Persian Bazaar manner with which you seem to handle everything else, something's gonna get missed. And I wouldn't be doing my duty if I allowed Dawson and Downey to spend more hours in jail than necessary because their attorney had predetermined the path of least resistance.

(*Pause.*)

KAFFEE. Wow. I'm sexually aroused, Commander. I'm not kidding.

JO. I don't think your clients murdered anybody.

KAFFEE. Well we'll just have to take their word for it, won't we?

JO. I mean, I don't think there was any intent.

KAFFEE. What are you basing this on?

JO. Instinct.

KAFFEE. Instinct? The doctor's report says Santiago died of asphyxiation brought on by acute lactic acidosis. And that the nature of the acidosis strongly suggests poisoning. I don't know what any of that means, but it sounds pretty bad.

JO. The doctor's wrong.

KAFFEE. What a relief. I was afraid I wouldn't be able to use the Liar, Liar, Pants on Fire Defense.

JO. Good one, that was funny.

KAFFEE. Thank you. Look. Rest assured, I'm completely on top of the situation with Dawson and Donnelly.

JO. Downey.

KAFFEE. —Downey.

JO. (*Picks up attaché.*) Right. I'll speak to your supervisor.

KAFFEE. I understand. You go straight up Pennsylvania Avenue, it's the big white house with pillars in front.

JO. Thanks.

KAFFEE. I don't think you'll have much luck, though.

JO. Why not?

KAFFEE. I was detailed by JAG, remember? Somebody over there's under the impression that I'm a good lawyer. (*Pause.*) So while I appreciate your interest and admire your enthusiasm, I think I can pretty much cover things myself at this point.

JO. Do you know what a Code Red is?

MARKINSON. (*Puts letter down on the table.*) I'm appalled, sir.

KAFFEE. No.

JO. What a pity. (*SHE exits.*)

(*LIGHTS up on Jessep's office.*)

JESSEP. You're appalled?

MARKINSON. Yes sir.

JESSEP. That's pretty strong language, Matthew, I mean, cool off before you work yourself into a lather. You're appalled? Santiago breaks the chain of command, reports to a civilian organization, tells tales on another Marine, another member of his unit, another member of his squad, for Christ's sake ... What the hell's goin' on over at Windward, Matthew?

MARKINSON. Colonel, I think it might be more appropriate if this discussion were held in private.

JESSEP. Are you suggesting that the fault lies with Lt. Kendrick?

MARKINSON. Executive Office Windward is one of the most stressful positions in this hemisphere. No one knows that better than I do. Lt. Kendrick doesn't have half the experience it takes to command that wall.

KENDRICK. I certainly beg your pardon, Captain, but I won't take the blame for Private Santiago.

MARKINSON. I'm not talking about Private Santiago. I'm talking about Private Santiago and Private Barnes, and Corporal McNally, and Corporal Eastman, and Gunnery Sergeant Hughes. You're doing something wrong, Lieutenant!

KENDRICK. My methods of leadership are what brought me to this base.

MARKINSON. Don't interrupt me, I'm still your superior officer.

JESSEP. And I'm yours, Matthew.

MARKINSON. Colonel, I've suggested it before and I'll suggest it again. Move Lt. Kendrick to the Leeward side of the base, where there's an ocean between our perimeter and the enemy. Let him cut his teeth there. And for Christ's sake, transfer Santiago outa here before he gets his ass kicked.

JESSEP. Transfer Santiago.

MARKINSON. Right away. Now, sir.

JESSEP. Yeah. Yeah. I suppose you're right. I suppose that's the thing to do. (*Closes folder.*) Wait. Wait. I got a better idea. Let's transfer the whole squad off the base. We better do that. Let's —on second thought—Windward. The whole Windward division, let's transfer 'em off the base. Jon, go on out there and get those boys down off the fence, they're packing their bags. Tom ...

TOM. (*Entering.*) Yes, sir?

JESSEP. Get the President on the phone, we're surrendering our position in Cuba.

(*TOM turns to exit.*)

JESSEP. Wait a minute!

(*TOM turns.*)

JESSEP. Don't call the President. Maybe that's the
wrong thing to do. Maybe we should consider this for a
second. Maybe, instead of surrendering the fight because a
Marine made a mistake, maybe we should train Santiago.
What do you think, I'm just spit-balling, but maybe we, as
officers, have a responsibility to this country to see that
the men charged with it's security are trained professionals.
Maybe we have that responsibility to other members of the
Corps. Yes, yes, I'm certain I once read something like
that. See, and now I'm trying to think about how I'd feel if
some Marine got hurt or killed because a Pfc. in my
command didn't know that the fuck he was doing. And I'm
trying to think about how the other members of his unit
might feel, putting their lives in the hands of a man they
can't count on ... and this brief meditation has brought me
around to thinking that your suggestion of transferring
Private Santiago off the base, while expeditious, and
certainly painless, might not be, in a manner of speaking,
the "American Way." Kendrick stays at Windward;
Santiago stays on the wall.
    MARKINSON. Colonel, that's a mistake. This
Santiago incident isn't gonna go away all by itself.
    JESSEP. Tom, thank you.

(*TOM exits.*)

JESSEP. Matthew, I believe I will have a word with
you alone for just a moment. Jonathan, you're dismissed.

Why don't you and I have dinner at the O-Club. Nineteen-thirty?

    KENDRICK. I'd be delighted, sir, thank you.

    JESSEP. That's all.

(KENDRICK exits.)

    JESSEP. Matthew sit, please.

    MARKINSON. Thank you, sir.

    JESSEP. What do you think of Kendrick?

    MARKINSON. He's a good man.

    JESSEP. I think he's kind of a weasel myself.

    MARKINSON. Yes sir.

    JESSEP. But he's an awfully good officer and in the end we see eye to eye on the most efficient way to run a Marine Corps unit. We're in the business of saving lives, Matthew. With every degree that we allow ourselves to move off the mark of perfection as officers more people die—that's a responsibility that I take pretty seriously. 'Cause I absolutely believe that simply taking a Marine who's not yet up to the job and packing him off to another assignment is the same as sending a kid into the jungle with a weapon that backfires.

(MARKINSON starts to stand.)

    JESSEP. Matthew, sit down. I'm younger than you are, Matthew, and if that's a source of tension or embarrassment for you, well, I don't give a shit. I'm in the business of saving lives, Captain Markinson. Don't ever question my orders in front of another officer.

(LIGHTS up on the Brig.)

    DAWSON. Officer on deck, ten-hut.

KAFFEE. Hi.

DAWSON. Sir. Lance Corporal Harold W. Dawson, sir.

KAFFEE. Someone hasn't been working and playing well with others, Harold.

DAWSON. Yes, sir.

DOWNEY. Sir, Private First Class Louden Downey, sir.

KAFFEE. I'm Daniel Kaffee, I'm your attorney. This is Sam Weinberg, he's from the A.C. Nielson Company, he's gonna talk to you about viewer preferences in the Carribean Command. You can sit down.

(*DOWNEY and DAWSON sit. KAFFEE takes out two signed affidavits and shows one to Dawson.*)

KAFFEE. Is this your signature?

DAWSON. Yes, sir.

KAFFEE. You don't have to call me sir. (*Then shows one to Downey.*) Is this your signature?

DOWNEY. Sir, yes, sir.

KAFFEE. And you certainly don't have to do it twice in one sentence. Either of you guys like baseball?

DAWSON. Sir?

KAFFEE. Really, you don't have to call me sir. I was just asking if you liked baseball.

DAWSON. Sir?

KAFFEE. What's a Code Red?

DAWSON. Sir, a Code Red is a disciplinary engagement.

KAFFEE. I don't understand.

DAWSON. Sir, a Marine falls out of line, it's up to the men in his unit to get him back on track.

KAFFEE. (*Pause.*) These disciplinary engagements occur often?

DAWSON. Yes, sir.

KAFFEE. What's a garden variety Code Red?

DAWSON. Sir?

KAFFEE. Harold, you say sir and I turn around and look for my father. Daniel, Danny, Dan, Kaffee—This can be fun, you know, it doesn't have to be unpleasant. Garden variety. Typical. What's a basic Code Red?

DAWSON. Sir, a Marine has refused to bathe on a regular basis. The men in his squad would give him a G.I. shower.

KAFFEE. What's that?

DAWSON. Scrub brushes, brillo pads, steel wool ...

SAM. Beautiful.

KAFFEE. The attack on Santiago was a disciplinary engagement.

DAWSON. Yes, sir.

KAFFEE. (*To Downey.*) Do you ever talk?

DAWSON. Lieutenant, Private Downey will answer any direct questions you ask him, sir.

KAFFEE. (*Pause.*) Swell. It says in the report you deny putting poison on the rag. What was it you were gonna do?

DOWNEY. Sir?

KAFFEE. What was his Code Red?

DOWNEY. We were gonna shave his hair, sir. We were just gonna shave his hair.

KAFFEE. When all of a sudden?

DAWSON. We saw blood dripping out of his mouth. We pulled the tape off his mouth and pulled the gag out, sir.

KAFFEE. Was there more blood?

DOWNEY. All down his face, sir. And then Corporal Dawson called the ambulance.

KAFFEE. Did anyone see you call the ambulance?

DAWSON. No, sir.

KAFFEE. Were you there when the ambulance got there?

DAWSON. Yes, sir. That's when we were taken under arrest, sir.

KAFFEE. I want to tell you guys about something called attorney/client privilege. It means that you can say anything you want to us in here, and we can't repeat it without your permission. It's against the law, we took an oath. You took the oath, didn't you, Sam?

SAM. Yeah.

KAFFEE. Sam took the oath.

SAM. My fingers were crossed.

KAFFEE. Sam—

SAM. I took the oath.

KAFFEE. So you can tell us, I need you to tell us ... Harold, did you assault Santiago with the intent of killing him?

DAWSON. No, sir.

KAFFEE. What was your intent?

DAWSON. To give Private Santiago a Code Red, sir.

KAFFEE. Why?

DAWSON. To train him, sir.

SAM. Train him to do what?

DAWSON. Train him to think of his unit before himself, sir. Train him to respect the Code.

SAM. What's the Code?

DAWSON. Unit, Corps, God, Country.

SAM. I beg your pardon?

DAWSON. Unit, Corps, God, Country.

SAM. That's what you're supposed to fight for?

KAFFEE. Sam, what's it matter what they're supposed to fight for?

SAM. Never mind.

DOWNEY. Unit, Corps, God, Country, sir. That's our Code.

SAM. Right.

KAFFEE. We'll be back. Is there anything you need? Books, paper, cigarettes, a ham sandwich?

DAWSON. Sir. No thank you, sir.

KAFFEE. Harold, there's a concept I think you better start warming up to. (*Picks case up off seat of chair.*)

DAWSON. Sir?

KAFFEE. I'm the only friend you've got.

(*LIGHTS up on Ross.*)

ROSS. Dan Kaffee.

KAFFEE. (*Shaking hands.*) Smilin' Jack Ross.

ROSS. Welcome to the big time.

KAFFEE. Don't flatter yourself.

ROSS. I hope for Dawson and Downey's sake, you practice law better than you play softball.

KAFFEE. (*Sits SL chair.*) Unfortunately for Dawson and Downey, I don't do anything better than I play softball. What're we talking about?

ROSS. They plead guilty to Manslaughter, I'll drop the Conspiracy and the Conduct Unbecoming. Twenty years, they'll be home in twelve.

KAFFEE. They called the ambulance, Jack.

ROSS. I don't care if they called the Avon Lady, they killed a Marine.

KAFFEE. Says who?

ROSS. I've got a doctor who says he's sure.

KAFFEE. Remarkable conclusion to reach, given that no poison showed in the autopsy.

ROSS. Are you a doctor?

KAFFEE. No, but if shouldn't be hard to round some up. It'll only take me four to six weeks. Meantime, I'll move for a postponement, how's that?

ROSS. Don't fuck around with this one, Danny. I can recommend eleven.

KAFFEE. Do you know what a Code Red is?

ROSS. Where do you get this shit, Gomer Pyle?

KAFFEE. A Marine steps out of line, his room's a little messy, his hair's too long, he breaks the Chain of Command and informs on another Marine ... apparently it's up to the men in his unit to give him a little punishment.

ROSS. Involuntary, they won't do more than ten.

KAFFEE. They kick him around or they shove him in a shower and scrub him down with steel wool ... they shave his head.

ROSS. I can't go lower than Involuntary.

KAFFEE. Tell me, from a public relations standpoint, what's the worst thing about this case? That these Code Reds go on all the time and no one ever reports them, or that it was a Puerto Rican that got killed?

ROSS. Involuntary. Eight to ten.

KAFFEE. Seven. Parole in 28 months.

ROSS. That's out of the question.

KAFFEE. Extra! Extra! Read all about it!

ROSS. You're not intimidating me, pal-o-mine.

KAFFEE. No? I thought it was working?

ROSS. (*Stands.*) You want seven years. I need more on Code Red.

KAFFEE. I'm going down to Cuba tomorrow. I'm gonna bring back a statement from this Jessep guy that's gonna tell you all you ever wanted to know about the subject. When I do, I'd like you to recommend the seven years. In exchange, I'll please guilty to Aggravated Assault and use what influence I have to convince my clients not to sell the movie rights.

(*ROSS laughs.*)

KAFFEE. Did I say something funny?

ROSS. We'll talk when you get back.

KAFFEE. Jack, do we have a deal?

ROSS. Work for it.

KAFFEE. Jack, do we have a deal?

ROSS. You don't know it yet, pal, but you're going to school tomorrow.

(*LIGHTS up on Kaffee's office. JO sits at his desk.*)

JO. Hi.

KAFFEE. Come on in.

JO. Thank you.

KAFFEE. Any luck getting me replaced?

JO. No. I spoke to a half-dozen people at Division. Is there anyone in this command that you don't either drink or play softball with?

KAFFEE. Jo, I have no inbred hostility toward you, I really don't. But if you ever speak to a client of mine again without my permission, I'll have you disbarred.

JO. I had authorization.

KAFFEE. You had authorization from *where?*

JO. Downey's closest living relative, Ginny Miller, his aunt on his mother's side. I thought sure it might be unethical, but as long as it wasn't illegal, what the hell.

KAFFEE. You got authorization from Aunt Ginny?

JO. I gave her a call. I thought she might be concerned. Perfectly within my province. You know what she said?

KAFFEE. You got authorization from Aunt Ginny.

JO. She said she's positive some mistake has been made.

KAFFEE. Does Aunt Ginny have a barn? We can hold the trial there. I can sew the costumes, and maybe his Uncle Goober could be the judge.

JO. I'll get out of your way now.

KAFFEE. Thank you.

JO. Was your father Lionel Kaffee?

KAFFEE. Yes.

JO. Really?

KAFFEE. I'm pretty sure.

JO. I've studied, you know, all his—I think he was one of the best trial lawyers—ever. I've read everything he's written. A lot.

(*Pause.*)

KAFFEE. Me, too.

JO. Right ... right ... (*Pause.*) You know what's odd?

KAFFEE. (*Pause.*) What's odd?

JO. At one-thirty, almost an hour after Santiago dies, the doctor, Commander Stone—couldn't determine the cause of death. But four hours later he said it was poison.

KAFFEE. (*Pause.*) Why ... of course ... I see what you mean ...

JO. Do you?

KAFFEE. It had to be Professor Plum with the Candlestick.

JO. Kaffee. Somewhere between 1:30 and 5:30, someone met with the doctor and told him to say it was poison. Someone coerced the doctor.

KAFFEE. Someone coerced the doctor. Do you work with a ouija board?

JO. I'm going down to Cuba with you tomorrow.

KAFFEE. No you're not.

JO. Yeah. I am. I called my office. They're sending me on an Observation and Evaluation field trip. Isn't that great?

KAFFEE. Is this what you meant by "I'll get out of your way now?"

(*SAM enters with two bottles of beer.*)

SAM. She's asleep now. When Laura gets back, you're my witness. The baby spoke. My daughter said a word.

KAFFEE. Your daughter made a sound. I'm not sure it was a word.

SAM. Oh come on, it was a word.

KAFFEE. Okay.

SAM. You heard her. The girl sat here, pointed, and said "Pa." She did, she said Pa.

KAFFEE. She was pointing at a doorknob.

SAM. That's right. Pointing as if to say "Pa, look, a doorknob."

KAFFEE. Samuel, why do two guys with the intent of killing someone call an ambulance when they see blood?

SAM. Why does anybody do anything?

KAFFEE. That's not good enough.

SAM. It's good enough for me.

KAFFEE. No it's not. Why do they call an ambulance when they see blood?

SAM. *You* say—

KAFFEE. *They* say they called the ambulance.

SAM. They panicked.

KAFFEE. I don't know about Downey, but Dawson's never panicked about anything in his life.

SAM. I think the clients are lucky you're lead counsel.

KAFFEE. You'd let the hammer drop?

SAM. I'd serve him to Division with a fuckin' cherry on top.

KAFFEE. Thank you, Judd for the defense. Have a good night.

SAM. Remember to wear your whites, it's hot down there.

KAFFEE. I don't look good in whites.

SAM. Nobody looks good in whites, but we're going to Cuba in July. You got Dramamine?

KAFFEE. Dramamine keeps you cool?

SAM. Dramamine keeps you from throwing up. You get sick when you fly.

KAFFEE. I get sick when I fly 'cause I'm afraid of crashing into a big mountain. I don't think Dramamine'll help.

SAM. I've got some oregano. I hear that works pretty good.

KAFFEE. Sam, did you know that there's only one piece of evidence linking them to the crime? It's their presence at the scene. They stood there and waited for the MPs to show up.

SAM. Ask them what they're supposed to fight for.

KAFFEE. Sam, they stood there and waited to be arrested.

SAM. Of course. These two people have a fierce sense of honor.

(*LIGHTS go up on a platoon meeting.*)

DUNN. Ten-hut.

KENDRICK. Report.

DUNN. Sir, Corporal Dunn, Alpha Squad present, sir.

THOMAS. Corporal Thomas, Bravo's present, sir.

HAMMAKER. Sir, Corporal Hammaker, sir, Charlie Squad's present.

DAWSON. Sir, Lance Corporal Dawson. Delta Squad's present less two.

KENDRICK. Report.

DAWSON. Pfc. Santiago and Pfc. Downey, sir.

KENDRICK. Private Santiago's been excused from the meeting, where's Downey?

DAWSON. Private Downey radioed in to the switch, sir, his jeep blew out. He and pick-up are making it back by foot.

KENDRICK. Pass on my words to Private Downey.

DAWSON. Yes, sir.

KENDRICK. Revelations II: I know thy works and thy labor and how thou canst not bare them which are evil. And thou hast tried them which say they are apostles and has found them to be liars. If you have a problem, and you're a Pfc., who do you take that problem to?

ALL. Sir, your Corporal, sir!

KENDRICK. If you have a problem, and you're a Corporal, who do you take that problem to?

ALL. Sir, your sergeant, sir!

KENDRICK. Private Santiago of Delta Squad has layed waste our priorities and made wretched our Code. Priorities:

ALL. Unit, Corps, God, Country!

KENDRICK. Code:

ALL. Unit, Corps, God, Country!!

KENDRICK. Priorities:

ALL. Unit, Corps, God, Country!!

KENDRICK. Code.

ALL. Unit, Corps, God, Country!!!

KENDRICK. Do you need someone from outside this unit to show you how to be good?

ALL. Sir no sir!

KENDRICK. Do you need someone from outside this unit to show you how to be right?

ALL. Sir no sir!

KENDRICK. Corporal Dunn.

DUNN. Sir.

KENDRICK. You think you and the boys of Alpha Squad could show Private Santiago how to be right?

DUNN. Sir yes sir.

KENDRICK. Anybody in Alpha goes near him, you'll answer to me, is that clear?

DUNN. Sir?

KENDRICK. Is it clear?

DUNN. Sir yes sir.

KENDRICK. Alpha's dismissed.

(*DUNN exits*)

KENDRICK. Corporal Thomas.

THOMAS. Sir!

KENDRICK. How 'bout my brave men of Bravo. I bet I turn this over to your boys and Santiago's a Marine by sunrise, am I right?

THOMAS. Sir yes sir!

KENDRICK. Bravo touches him and you'll all be filling sandbags till you beg for mercy. Dismissed.

(*THOMAS exits.*)

KENDRICK. Corporal Hammaker.

HAMMAKER. Sir!

KENDRICK. I have two things to say to you. The first is that I believe in my heart that you and the men of Charlie Squad are outstanding Marines and that your influence over the Private would be invaluable. The second is that the government of the United States maintains a military installation in the Arctic Circle, and you and the men of Charlie will find yourselves scraping icicles off of igloos in a heartbeat if you so much as look funny at the private. Is that clear?

HAMMAKER. Yes sir!

KENDRICK. No Code Reds, is that clear?

HAMMAKER. Sir yes sir!

KENDRICK. No Code Reds, is that clear?!

HAMMAKER. Sir yes sir!
KENDRICK. NO CODE REDS, IS THAT CLEAR?!!
HAMMAKER. Sir yes sir!!!
KENDRICK. DISMISSED.

(*HAMMAKER exits.*
KENDRICK stands next to Dawson; BOTH facing front.)

KENDRICK. Lance Corporal Dawson. (*Turns his head to Dawson.*)

(*LIGHTS up on Santiago's room.*
SANTIAGO is dragged on by DOWNEY. HIS hands and feet are tied with rope and HIS eyes are covered with duct tape. DAWSON joins them.)

SANTIAGO. HEEELLLP MEEEE!!!!!

(*DOWNEY holds Santiago's head back as DAWSON stuffs a piece of white cotton cloth into his mouth.*)

DAWSON. This is my job, Private, okay? It's my responsibility. I've gotta train you how to be right. You're a Marine and you've got honor. You can't make mistakes, Private, you don't make mistakes. Not while you're in my squad. The Corps helps those who help themselves.
DOWNEY. (*Has a roll of dull, grey duct tape.*) You're lucky it's us, Willy. Could be worse. Could be somebody else. (*Tears off a piece of duct tape and wraps it around Santiago's mouth.*)

(*BLACKOUT.*
A PLATOON OF MARINES is heard chanting during which the set changes.)

MARINES. (*Chanting.*).
LIFT YOUR HEAD AND LIFT IT HIGH
Lift your head and lift it high
DELTA COMPANY'S PASSIN' BY
Delta Company's passin' by ...
I DON'T KNOW BUT I'VE BEEN TOLD
I don't know but I've been told
ALL MARINES ARE MIGHTY BOLD
All Marines are mighty bold

(*The chanting continues over the sounds of JETS taking off and landing.*)

MARINES CHANT.
SOUND OFF—
One Two!
SOUND OFF—
Three Four!
SOUND OFF—
One Two Three Four
ONE TWO—
Three Four!

(*The sound of JETS continue as HOWARD, a Marine, crosses to meet KAFFEE, JO and SAM as they enter. We're on a landing strip. ALL are wearing dark glasses. KAFFEE and SAM are dressed in summer whites; JO in khakis. The SUN shines very bright in Guantanamo Bay.*)

HOWARD. (*Shouting over the noise.*) Lieutenants Kaffee and Weinberg?
KAFFEE. (*Shouting.*) Yeah.
JO. Commander Galloway.

HOWARD. Corporal Howard, ma'am. I'm to escort you to the Windward side of the base.

JO. Thank you.

HOWARD. I have some camouflage jackets in the jeep, sirs, I'll have to ask you both to put them on.

KAFFEE. Camouflage jackets?

HOWARD. Yes sir. Regulations. We'll be riding pretty close to the fence, sir. The Cubans see an officer in white, they think it's someone they might wanna take a shot at .

KAFFEE. Good call, Sam.

HOWARD. The jeep's right over there, ma'am. We'll just hop on the ferry and be there in no time.

KAFFEE. We have to take a boat?

HOWARD. Yes, sir. To get to the other side of the bay.

KAFFEE. Whitaker didn't say anything about a boat.

HOWARD. Is there a problem, sir?

KAFFEE. No. No problem. I'm just not crazy about boats.

JO. Jesus Christ, Kaffee, you're in the Navy for cryin' out loud, you wanna get a hold of yourself?

KAFFEE. (*Crossing to Howard, shouting.*) Nobody likes her very much.

HOWARD. Yes sir.

(*LIGHTS up on Jessep's office.*)

JESSEP. Nathan Jessep, come on in and siddown.

KAFFEE. (*Shake hands.*) Thank you. I'm Daniel Kaffee. This is Commander Jo Galloway, she's observing and evaluating—

JO. How do you do? (*Shake hands.*)

JESSEP. Pleased to meet you Commander.

KAFFEE. Sam Weinberg, he has no responsibilities here whatsoever.

JESSEP. I've asked Captain Markinson and Lt. Kendrick to join us. Matthew's Company Commander and Jonathan's X.O. for the Windward side. Gentlemen, meet Lieutenants Kaffee and Weinstein—

SAM. Weinberg.

JESSEP. And Commander Galloway.

KENDRICK. How do you do?

MARKINSON. Lt. Kaffee, I had the pleasure of meeting your father once. I was a teenager and he spoke at my high school.

(*KAFFEE smiles and nods.*)

JESSEP. Lionel Kaffee?

KAFFEE. Yes sir.

JESSEP. Well, Jimminy Goddamn Cricket. Jonathan, you're too young to know, but this man's dad once made a lot of enemies down in your neck of the woods. Jefferson vs. Madison County School District. Folks down there said a little negro boy couldn't go to a white school. Lionel said we'll see about that. How the hell is your dad?

KAFFEE. I'm sorry sir?

JESSEP. Still trying to overthrow the Government?

KAFFEE. Not any longer, sir.

JESSEP. Oh, no, did he pass away?

KAFFEE. Yes sir.

JESSEP. I'm sorry, son.

KAFFEE. Thank you, sir. It was seven years ago.

JESSEP. (*Pause.*) Well ... don't I feel like the fuckin' asshole.

KAFFEE. Not at all, sir.

JESSEP. What can we do for you, Danny.

KAFFEE. Actually, Colonel, quite a bit. One letter from you or your officers could go a long way toward reducing the boys sentences.

JESSEP. A letter saying what, Danny?

KAFFEE. Saying that Code Reds are a practiced custom on the base, and that Dawson and Downey, otherwise exceptional Marines, were simply disciplining one of their own when an accident happened.

JESSEP. I have some tragic news for you, Danny.

KAFFEE. What's that, Colonel?

JESSEP. You made the long trek to Cuba for nothing.

KAFFEE. Well, I think if you give me ten minutes of your time, I can persuade you.

JESSEP. Jon, check your watch.

(*KENDRICK looks at his watch.*)

JESSEP. Go.

(*LIGHTS up on Santiago.*)

SANTIAGO. Dear Senator, I have written to you before on my problems with my unit here in Cuba. I am threatened or picked on almost every day by the members of my own unit. They write me up on charges of malingering and say that I'm making believe I'm sick. I fainted during a run and asked to go to the doctor and they paid no attention. I've been warned by a friend to keep quiet 'cause they're looking for any little detail so they can write me up. I do not want to be part of any unit or organization who endangers the lives of their men just by training them. Please help me resolve this problem. Or if I could call you sir, I could explain it a lot better.

(*LIGHTS up on Jessep's office. The meeting continues.*)

JESSEP. Danny, this was no Code Red.

KAFFEE. Well, that's really a matter of—

JESSEP. No, Danny, I'm sorry, I really am. Lt. Kendrick told the men specifically not to give Santiago a Code Red.

KAFFEE. When was this?

KENDRICK. Sixteen-hundred hours. Seven-July.

MARKINSON. We had a meeting here. And then Lt. Kendrick spoke to 2nd platoon.

KENDRICK. We anticipated the Code Red, and we tried to prevent it.

JESSEP. Code Reds are a privilege. Code Reds are for those worth the time. Santiago was a weak link and he was dangerous. He wasn't worth the time and the men knew I felt that way.

KAFFEE. How would they know that, sir?

JESSEP. Because as soon as I saw the letter, I ordered his immediate transfer off the base.

KAFFEE. Santiago was about to be transferred?

JESSEP. At oh-two-hundred that morning. Two hours too late as it turned out, 'cause at midnight, your clients stuck a rag soaked with anti-freeze down his throat.

JO. Sir, the boys say there was no poison on the rag.

KAFFEE. Jo.

JESSEP. The doctor says there was.

KAFFEE. Colonel, do you still have a copy of the transfer order?

JESSEP. Right here.

KAFFEE. Could I hold on to that?

JESSEP. Now what's that supposed to mean?

KAFFEE. I'm sorry?

JESSEP. How am I supposed to feel about that?

KAFFEE. Oh, jeez, I didn't mean to imply that—

JESSEP. Of course you did.

KAFFEE. No sir, it's a matter of collecting—

JESSEP. I was feeling very friendly toward you and your team of lawyers, when mistrust reared its ugly head.

KAFFEE. Mistrust is the farthest thing from—

JESSEP. Of course you can have a copy of the order. I'm here to help anyway I can.

KAFFEE. Thank you, sir.

JESSEP. You believe that, don't you? That I'm here to help any way I can?

KAFFEE. Of course.

JESSEP. I have three copies of that order, and more than happy to let you have one.

KAFFEE. It's just—

JESSEP. But you have to ask me nicely.

KAFFEE. (*Pause.*) I beg your pardon.

JESSEP. You have to ask me nicely.

KAFFEE. Sir, may I please have—

JO. What the hell kinda garbanzo nonsense is this?

KAFFEE. Jo.

JO. We don't work for you, Colonel, we're investigating a crime.

KAFFEE. We are not investigating a crime.

JESSEP. Joanne, you seem a trifle perturbed. How about a gumball?

JO. No thank you, sir. I wonder if I could ask you a question, though.

KAFFEE. No.

JESSEP. Name it.

JO. Between 1:30 and 5:30 on the morning of the 8th, did you meet with Dr. Stone?

KAFFEE. Commander, the Colonel doesn't need to answer that.

JO. Of course he does.

KAFFEE. No, he really doesn't.

JO. Yeah, he really does. Colonel?

JESSEP. You know, it just sunk in. She outranks him. (*To Kaffee.*) She outranks you.

KAFFEE. (*Pause.*) Yes, sir.

JESSEP. I want to tell you something and listen up, 'cause I mean this: You're the luckiest man in the world. There is, believe me, gentlemen, nothing sexier on earth than a woman you have to salute in the morning. Promote 'em all, I say, 'cause this is true: If you've never gotten a blow-job from a superior office, then you are letting the best of life just pass you by.

JO. Did you consult with the doctor that night?

KAFFEE. Back off, Commander.

JESSEP. You see, my problem is, of course, that I'm a Lt. Colonel. I'll have to keep taking cold showers till they elect some gal President.

JO. I need an answer to my question, Colonel.

JESSEP. You'll get an answer.

JO. I need it now, sir.

JESSEP. Take caution in your tone, Commander. I'm a fair guy. But this fuckin' heat's making me absolutely crazy. Yes, of course I had a meeting with the doctor. One of my men was dead.

JO. Thank you, sir.

KAFFEE. Hey, listen, we'll get outa your hair. I just need a piece of paper that says Santiago died due to an accident that occurred during a Code Red.

KENDRICK. Lt. Kaffee, I believe in God, and in His son, Jesus Christ. And because I do, I can say this: Private Santiago isn't dead because of a Code Red. He's dead because he had no honor. He's dead because he had no Code. And God was watching.

SAM. (*To Jo.*) How do you feel about that theory?

KAFFEE. Sam.

KENDRICK. I don't like you people.

SAM. Look at this, another Christmas card I'm not gonna get.

KAFFEE. That's it! The two of you, wait outside.

SAM. I apologize.

KAFFEE. Wait outside. (*To Jo.*) You too.

JO. (*Stands and looks at Jessep.*) Please excuse us.

JESSEP. Joanne. How about I shut my eyes and pretend I'm just a Chief Petty Officer. You've still got an hour before your plane leaves, what do you say?

JO. (*Turns to Jessep.*) What would I do with the other 59 minutes, Colonel?

(*SHE and SAM exit.*)

KAFFEE. Colonel, however you may feel about the value of these Code Reds or the intent of my clients, on the night of the seventh, the fact is, none of it looks very good to the outside world. Now, I can't detain you or charge you with a crime, but on a slow news day, I could sure as hell piss on your National Security Council seat. So what I'm saying is this. Why don't you let me be your attorney. I'll draft a statement and I'll make sure you're safe. Meanwhile, (*Pulls his chair in close next to Jessep.*) my guys get a break and everybody's happy.

(*HE sits resting his hands on the table.*)

JESSEP. Danny?

KAFFEE. Yes sir.

JESSEP. Did I just hear you threaten me?

KAFFEE. I was laying out a possible option, sir.

JESSEP. I don't think so. I think I heard you threatening me. I think you thought you were gonna walk in here and flash a badge and that was gonna mean something. I eat breakfast seventy yards away from 3,000 Cubans who are trained to kill me.

(*KAFFEE removes his hands from the table as JESSEP slams his hand down on the table.*)

JESSEP. Danny, believe this. I'd kill you. I'd kill
everyone in this room. I'd kill anyone to protect what I am
paid to protect. Go home, back behind the lines. Go home
where your white uniform won't get you killed. Give in to
what I'm saying. You believe every word. Lt. Kendrick?
KENDRICK. Ten minutes.
JESSEP. Meeting's over, Navy. Anchors Aweigh.

(*KAFFE stands and moves to leave.*)

JESSEP. Daniel. Transfer order.

KAFFEE. (*Turns to Jessep who offers him a copy of the
transfer order.*) No. (*Beat.*) No, I don't need it.

(*LIGHTS up outside Jessep's office.*)

SAM. I believe in God and in his son, Jesus Christ?
Good, we'll just take that gun out of your hands now.

(*KAFFEE enters, HE's aggitated.*)

JO. What happened in there?
KAFFEE. Nothing.
JO. What do you mean nothing?
KAFFEE. Nothing. Nothing happened.
JO. Will he give you a statement?
KAFFEE. No. I'll come up with something else.
HOWARD. (*Salutes.*) Excuse me, sir—
KAFFEE. What?
HOWARD. These are your security tags for the flight
back. They got your flight code.
KAFFEE. (*Takes tags.*) Thank you.

HOWARD. Yep. It's an AF-40 transport. It doesn't have any windows, but it flies.

KAFFEE. (*Gives security tags to SAM/JO, who attach them to their cases.*) I'm sure it'll be fine.

HOWARD. It doesn't have any windows, but it gets you there.

KAFFEE. The AF-40 is fine. (*Kneels DC and attaches security tag to his case.*)

HOWARD. You better be sure and keep them tags secure, sir. You don't want to lose 'em. The boys out at the strip like to hassle you navy people now and again when they get the shot.

SAM. Why? What'd we ever do to them?

HOWARD. Oh, nothin', sir. The navy's been great, sir. Every time we gotta go someplace and fight, you boys always give us a ride.

KAFFEE. Get the jeep.

HOWARD. Yes sir. I'll be back tout-suite. (*HE does an about-face and exits.*)

KAFFEE. Listen, Jo. (*Pause.*) I made a joke the other day about being sexually aroused. I'm sorry. It was rude and unprofessional.

JO. (*Pause.*) Bet your ass, sugar bear.

KAFFEE. You've observed, you've evaluated, it's over. Tomorrow morning they'll be arraigned, and if I can work up something fast, they'll get Aggravated Assault, and that's the end of it. (*Puts on his hat and dark glasses and exits DL.*)

(*SAM stands and follows.*)

SAM. "You boys always give us a ride." ... I wonder how long he's been working on that one. (*Turns to Jo.*) I hate this place. (*THEY exit.*)

(*LIGHTS up on Jessep's office.*)

JESSEP. "First thing we do, let's kill all the lawyers."
MARKINSON. (*Pause.*) Shakespeare.
JESSEP. I hate casualties, Matthew. A Marine smothers a grenade and saves his platoon, that Marine's doing his job. There are casualties. Even in victory. (*Stands.*) The fabric of this base, the foundation of the unit, the spirit of the Corps, these things are worth fighting for. And there's no one who doesn't know that who's ever made the choice to put on the uniform. I hate casualties. (*Pause.*) Dawson and Downey, they're smothering a grenade.
MARKINSON. Just the same, sir, if I were you, I'd get myself a lawyer.

(*LIGHTS OUT.*)

MARINES. (*Chanting.*)
WHAT'RE YOU GONNA DO WHEN YOU GET BACK?!
What're you gonna do when you get back?
TAKE A SHOWER AND HIT THE RACK!
Take a shower and hit the rack!
OH NO
Not me
OH NO
Not us.
What're we gonna do when we get back
Polish up for a sneak attack

(*LIGHTS up on Brig.*)

DAWSON. Officer on deck, ten-hut.

(*KAFFEE enters.*)

KAFFEE. Why did you care that Santiago was writing a letter?

DAWSON. Sir?

KAFFEE. I want to know why you cared?

DAWSON. It was a Code Red, sir.

KAFFEE. Colonel Jessep thinks you're fulla shit. He doesn't think you were just trying to train Santiago. He thinks you were trying to kill him.

DOWNEY. That's not true, sir—

DAWSON. Private, the Lieutenant didn't ask for an opinion.

KAFFEE. What's true? Why did you care?

DAWSON. It was a Code Red, sir.

KAFFEE. Eight thousand men on that base, why did you care?

DAWSON. I was his Squad Leader, sir. It was my job, sir.

KAFFEE. Yeah, but why did you care?

DAWSON. Private Santiago broke the —

KAFFEE. Not you. Him. Why did you care?

DOWNEY. Sir, Private Santiago broke the—

KAFFEE. No, no, I don't want to hear about your chain of command, I don't want to hear about your loyalty. I don't wanna hear about your bozo code of honor. Why did you care?

DOWNEY. Sir, Private Santiago broke—

KAFFEE. *Did you hear what I just said??!!*

DOWNEY. Private Santiago needed to learn how to—

KAFFEE. Why did you care??!!

DOWNEY. He—a weak link—we have a responsibility—

KAFFEE. Bullshit! Why did you care?!!!

DAWSON. Because God was watching.

(*KAFFEE—stopped in his tracks.*)

KAFFEE. What did Kendrick say to you?

(*The platoon meeting.*
DAWSON turns to face Kendrick.)

KENDRICK. God is watching, Lance Corporal Dawson. And he helps those who help themselves. And so do I. Get your house in order, Lance Corporal. Unit, Corps, God, Country ... and duty to self simply isn't part of the equation. Get your house in order, so that these men can believe in you again. Get your house in order ... so that the Lord our God can look down and say "There is a United States Marine and I will stand at his side." Get your house in order ... and don't let anybody ever tell you we're not at war. (*Pause.*) Would you like me to tell you what to do now?
DAWSON. Sir, yes sir.

(*LIGHTS up on the Brig.*)

KAFFEE. You were given an order.
DAWSON. Yes, sir.
KAFFEE. Lt. Kendrick gave you an order to give Santiago a Code Red.
DAWSON. Yes, sir.
KAFFEE. You mind telling me why the hell you never mentioned this before?
DAWSON. You didn't ask us, sir.
KAFFEE. Cutie-pie shit's not gonna win you a place in my heart, Corporal. I get paid no matter how much time you spend in jail.
DAWSON. Yes, sir. I know you do, sir.

KAFFEE. Fuck you, Harold. (*Pause.*) Here's what's gonna happen. You'll swear out deposition against Kendrick, saying that he ordered the Code Red. If you do, I think I can get a good deal. I think I can get six months. (*Pause* "Wow, Kaffee, you're the greatest lawyer in the world, how can we ever thank you?" Fellas, I just told you you're gonna go home in six months.

DAWSON. Sir, permission to speak.

KAFFEE. Speak.

DAWSON. Begging the Lieutenant's pardon—

KAFFEE. What??!!

DAWSON. I'm afraid we can't do that, sir.

KAFFEE. (*Pause.*) Can't do what?

DAWSON. Make a deal, sir. I'm afraid I can't say that Lieutenant Kendrick ordered the Code Red.

KAFFEE. (*Pause.*) Look, are you telling me the truth? About the meeting?

DAWSON. Yes, sir.

KAFFEE. But you won't say so in a written statement?

DAWSON. Not so we can make a deal, I'm afraid not, sir.

KAFFEE. (*Pause.*) Why?

DAWSON. We live by a Code, sir. Either we were right or we were wrong. We don't make deals.

KAFFEE. Well zippity doo-dah. You don't turn Government evidence, the best I can get you is seven years.

DAWSON. That's fine, sir.

KAFFEE. No, that's not fine, you pompous asshole. I'm offering you six months!

DAWSON. What do we do then, sir?

KAFFEE. When?

DAWSON. After six months, sir. What do we do after six months?

KAFFEE. (*Pause.*) I'm talking to you about—

DAWSON. We didn't join 'cause we felt like it. We joined 'cause it was a life decision. We wanted to live by a Code, sir. And we found it in the Corps. And now you're asking me to sign a piece of paper that says we have no honor. We have no Code. You're asking us to say we're not Marines. (*Pause.*) We're being tested. And if we fail, I'm asking you, sir, with all due respect for your Lieutenant's bars, what do we do after six months?

(*KAFFEE/DAWSON stare each other down for a long moment.*)

KAFFEE. You guys are a freak show.

(*Outside Brig.*)

JO. (*Enters DR and crosses to Kaffee.*) What'd they say?
KAFFEE. Are you just following me around 24 hours a day?
JO. Markinson resigned his commission.
KAFFEE. What?
JO. Captain Markinson resigned his commission.
KAFFEE. (*Pause.*) When?
JO. Tonight. After we left.
KAFFEE. I'll get in touch with him tomorrow.
JO. I already tried. I can't find him. What'd they say?
KAFFEE. Jo, this really comes under the heading of none of your business.
JO. I'm Louden Downey's attorney. Aunt Ginny. She feels like she's known me for years. She said she'd feel very comfortable if I were directly involved in the case. Louden signed the papers an hour ago. (*Hands Kaffee a folder.*) I'd appreciate it, by the way, if you didn't speak to my client without my permission. But since you did, what'd they say?

KAFFEE. You make me nervous, Joanne. (*Hands folder back to Jo.*) I'm involved in a situation in which the stakes couldn't be higher. I'm not gonna take time out to give tutorials in criminal procedure to a restless dilettante with a gut feeling.

JO. That was a nice speech. What'd they say?

KAFFEE. Kendrick gave them an order.

JO. What do we do now?

KAFFEE. Find Jack Ross.

(*LIGHTS up on conference room. The argument's pretty heated.*)

ROSS. You *talk* to the other guys in the platoon.

KAFFEE. I don't need to—

ROSS. Alpha, Bravo, Charlie, they all say the same thing. Kendrick specifically said not to *touch* Santiago.

KAFFEE. They weren't there, he dismissed the platoon. You talk to *Kendrick*.

ROSS. I already talked to Kendrick, he denies everything.

JO. You talked to Kendrick? Why did you think there was anything to deny?

KAFFEE. Joanne—

ROSS. I had a suspicion.

JO. You had a —

KAFFEE. It's not important now.

(*SAM sits.*)

JO. You had a suspicion? And you chose not to share it with anyone?

ROSS. It was just a sus—

JO. You're in violation of about fourteen articles of the Code of Ethics.

KAFFEE. This is Joanne Galloway, she's very pleased to meet you.

ROSS. Ebenezer Galloway?

KAFFEE. She's Downey's attorney.

JO. And you're about thirty seconds away from a felony evidence tampering charge.

ROSS. You wanna *charge* me with something?

JO. How long were you gonna—

KAFFEE. Jo, this is another one of those situations.

JO. No, no, no, you ask him how he's getting his information 12, 24, 72 hours before we—

ROSS. You wanna *charge* me with something, lady?!

SAM. (*Stands.*) Let's settle down, huh?

ROSS. Please, I'm begging you, charge me with something.

SAM. Hey!! In the interest of justice, everybody take a deep knee bend.

(*THEY take a break for a moment.*)

ROSS. Kendrick had a platoon meeting. He told the men what Santiago had done. And he told them that Santiago *was not* to get a Code Red. I have Kendrick's deposition, as well as the depositions of every other man at that meeting.

KAFFEE. Kendrick's lying, Jack.

ROSS. (*Pause.*) I think you're right. (*Pause.*) I think he's lying. (*Pause.*) But so what? Neither of us can prove it. (*Pause.*)

KAFFEE. I'm not sure about that. Why does a Marine Captain resign his commission after twenty-one years?

ROSS. We'll never know.

KAFFEE. You don't think I can subpoena Markinson?

ROSS. You can try, but you won't find him. You know what Markinson did for the first seventeen of his twenty-one years in the Corps? C.I.C., Danny, counter-intelligence. Markinson's gone. There is no Markinson.

(*The wind has been taken out of Kaffee's sails.*)

ROSS. RSC is an effective unit. And Lt. Colonel Jessep's star is on the rise. They'll let me bend over backwards to spare that base, and the Corps, any embarrassment. (*Pause.*) So this is it. Aggravated Assault. Seven years. All things considered, it's not a bad week's work for the defense.

JO. He's bluffing. He's got a p.r. problem and he can't afford to go to court.

KAFFEE. Commander, every time you open your mouth you're taking years off the client's lives! Now shut up!! (*Pause.*) I'm sorry, Jack.

ROSS. No, she's absolutely right. I can't afford to go to court. Lucky for you, huh, Danny? You're turning green at the thought of it. No, taking this to court would be bad for me. It'd be bad for the Marine Corps and I'd be held responsible. But *you* go to court, and the boys go away for thirty years.

KAFFEE. Jack—

ROSS. Are we *clear* on that?! We *have* to be clear on that. Once we go outside this room, I have to go all the way, they'll be charged with murder. And in a courtroom, you lose this case. Please. I'm the Judge Advocate and I'm telling you I don't think your guys belong in jail. (*Pause.*) But I don't get to make that decision. I represent the People. Without passion. You see? And the People have a case. (*To Kaffee.*) If you could get me written statements from the defendants, they'd do six months. Without the statements, it's seven years. Believe a thing this woman tells you, and they won't see the light of day 'till they're fifty-nine. That's the end of this negotiation. From this moment, we're on the record. Tomorrow morning, 9:45. I'll see you at the arraignment. (*He exits.*)

JO. Can I speak now?

KAFFEE. I'm not gonna talk to Dawson anymore. He won't take the deal. He doesn't like me. He's gonna go to jail just to spite me. So my job is done.

JO. I'm not talking about a deal.

KAFFEE. I won't have this conversation—

JO. Sam?

SAM. It's an unwinnable case. Let's take the seven years and run. It's a gift.

KAFFEE. It's not a gift. I won those seven years.

JO. Keep telling yourself that.

KAFFEE. What do you want from me?

JO. Why are you so afraid to be a lawyer?

KAFFEE. Jesus—

JO. Were daddy's expectations really that high?

SAM. Hey—

KAFFEE. Commander, Downey's your client. If you wanna take him into—

JO. Go to hell. Go to hell for saying that when you know I need Dawson and you know I need you. They think they were right. Let 'em be judged. Don't make the deal, make the argument. Let 'em be judged by a jury in a courtroom. Tell Dawson you want to plead Not Guilty. Tell Dawson you're going to make his argument for him.

SAM. An argument that didn't work for Calley at My Lai and an argument that didn't work for the Nazis at Nuremberg.

KAFFEE. For Christ sake, Sam, do you really think that's the same as two teenage Marines executing a routine order that they never believed would result in harm? I don't represent the Nazis, they're not my problem tonight.

(*Pause.*)

JO. That's right. (*Pause.*) So what're you gonna do? (*Pause.*) Danny?

KAFFEE. I'm sorry. Ross is right. In a courtroom we lose this case.

JO. That's not—

KAFFEE. I can't jeopardize what we have.

JO. But you know they're right. (*Pause.*) You know it.

KAFFEE. I know the law. (*Pause.*)

JO. (*Stands.*) You know nothing about the law. You're a used car salesman, Daniel, you're an ambulance chaser with a rank. You're nothing. Live with that. (*Exits.*)

(*SAM and KAFFEE remain silent a moment.*)

KAFFEE. Sam?

(*SAM turns front.*)

KAFFEE. Why does a junior grade with six months experience and a track record for plea bargaining get detailed for a murder case? (*Pause.*) Would it be to make sure that it never sees the inside of a courtroom?

(*LIGHTS out/Transition.*)

MARINES. (*Chanting.*)
UP IN THE MORNING WITH THE RISING SUN
Up in the morning with the rising sun
GONNA RUN ALL DAY TILL THE DAY IS DONE
Gonna run all day till the day is done
LEFT RIGHT
One Two
GO RIGHT
Three Four

LEFT RIGHT
One Two Three Four
One Two
Three Four!

(*The Brig as KAFFEE enters.*
KAFFEE has been drinking. DAWSON hears Kaffee and
wakes up. It's late at night.)

KAFFEE. They've got you guys in separate cells now, huh.

DAWSON. Yes, sir. (*Pause.*)

KAFFEE. You wanna hear a joke? (*Pause.*) You hear about the Japanese pilot who hated jazz? (*Pause.*) He bombed Pearl Bailey. (*Pause.*) I was ninety-nine percent sure you weren't gonna laugh at that. (*Takes out flask.*) You want some milk? Good for the teeth and bones.

DAWSON. No. Thank you, sir.

KAFFEE. (*Takes a drink and sits.*) Well ... I don't know how else to say this ... I think you gotta do it. Let me make a deal for you. (*Pause.*) I mean ... in the end ... what difference does it make? (*Pause.*)

DAWSON. Do you think we were right, sir?

KAFFEE. It doesn't matter what I think.

DAWSON. You're my lawyer. You need to tell me if I broke the law.

KAFFEE. It's not a matter of right and wrong—

DAWSON. Yes it is, it always is. (*Stands.*) That's something people like you say. But it is. If we were wrong, tell me, I'll accept that. But if we were right, I won't make a deal.

KAFFEE. (*Pause.*) What do you mean, people like me?

DAWSON. Do you think we're guilty?

KAFFEE. (*Pause.*) I think you'd lose.

DAWSON. You're such a coward. I can't believe they let you wear a uniform.

KAFFEE. (*Wheels around and punches Dawson in the stomach.*) You're going to Levenworth and there's nothing I can do it. I could've gotten you six months,

(*DAWSON straightens up.*)

KAFFEE. but you wouldn't let me. You're goin' to Levenworth for seven years and there's nothing I can do about it. (*Shouts off SL.*) MP! (*MP enters. KAFFEE moves to leave, then looks back at Dawson.*) What happened to saluting an officer when he leaves the room?

(*DAWSON stands for a moment, then takes his hands, puts them in his pockets and turns to the MP.*)

(*LIGHTS fade out on Brig.*
LIGHTS up on courtroom.
The SERGEANT AT ARMS enters and sets files, pen, and gavel with striker on table for Judge Randolph.
IN SINGLE FILE, MP, followed by DAWSON, DOWNEY—BOTH in handcuffs—and another MP enter and take their places.
ROSS enters and goes to his table. Then JO and SAM enter, move to their table and sit.
KAFFEE enters and moves to the defense table without looking at anyone.
As SERGEANT AT ARMS re-enters, JUDGE RANDOLPH follows.)

SERGEANT AT ARMS. Ten-hut.

(*EVERYONE stands. JUDGE RANDOLPH sits and strikes gavel.*)

JUDGE RANDOLPH. All right, where are we?

SERGEANT AT ARMS. Docket number 41 1275. VR-5. United States versus Lance Corporal Harold W. Dawson and Private First Class Louden Downey. Defendants are charged with Conspiracy to Commit Murder, Murder in the Second Degree, and Conduct Unbecoming A United States Marine.

JUDGE RANDOLPH. For the defense?

KAFFEE. Kaffee, Lt. Junior Grade Daniel Abernathy, United States Naval Reserve, Judge Advocate General's Corps. Sworn and certified in accordance with Articles 42a and 27b of the Uniform Code of Military Justice.

JUDGE RANDOLPH. Does defense wish to enter a plea?

KAFFEE. Yeah. (*Stands.*) They're not guilty.

(*The silence in the courtroom is broken by the sound of ROSS dropping his files into his briefcase and snapping it closed. As soon as this happens, we begin to hear a slow steady DRUM cadence which will continue until end of the Act.*)

JUDGE RANDOLPH. Enter a plea of Not Guilty for the defendants. We'll adjourn until ten hundred, one week from today, at which time this court will reconvene as a general court-martial. I'll see counsel in my chambers. Now. (*Raps gavel.*)

SERGEANT AT ARMS. Ten-hut..

(*ALL stand. JUDGE RANDOLPH exits.*)

KAFFEE. (*Holding his case as DOWNEY and DAWSON stop C with MPs.*) Say, boys.

DOWNEY. Yes, sir?

KAFFEE. Don't look at me and say, "yes sir", like I just asked you if you cleaned the latrine. You're not in the Marines anymore, you're in jail. Get some rest and don't speak to anyone. They're dismissed.

(*The MPs take the DEFENDANTS off.*)

KAFFEE. (*Pause.*) So this is what a courtroom looks like.

(*LIGHTS OUT/LIGHT UP on the Sentry Tower.*
Night. A THUNDERSTORM. The SENTRY stands
watch. A deafening clap of THUNDER.
BLACKOUT.)

End of ACT I

ACT II

LIGHTS up on JO, SAM and KAFFEE. ALL in same positions as at the end of ACT I.

SAM. No, listen to me—
KAFFEE. Sam—
SAM. Danny—
KAFFEE. Wait a second—
SAM. You haven't thought it through.
KAFFEE. They have a defense. They were following an order.
SAM. An illegal order.
KAFFEE. The fuck you think these guys know what an illegal order is? I don't know what an illegal order is.
SAM. Just hang on—
KAFFEE. They're not permitted to question orders. Period.
SAM. Then what's the secret? What're the magic words? I give orders every day and nobody follows them.
KAFFEE. Sam we have softball games and marching bands. They stand on a wall. They were ordered to do something that's routine down there. It's what they're taught to do.
SAM. The law says you can't do what they did, it's as simple as that.
KAFFEE. It's not as simple as that. We're defense counsel. We position the truth. What did they teach you?
SAM. To tell the truth, not position it.
KAFFEE. They taught you wrong. Talk to your friend at NIS, see what the deal is on Markinson.
SAM. I already did.

KAFFEE. And?

SAM. She said if Markinson doesn't want to be found we're not gonna find him. She said I could be Markinson and you wouldn't know it.

JO. Are you Markinson?

SAM. Commander.

JO. I'm not Markinson. That's two down.

KAFFEE. Find him. We'll meet at my apartment every night, seven o'clock. (*To Jo.*) I want you working with Downey two hours a day. Get him to stop squinting when the talks, he looks shifty. Sam, you're in charge of Dawson. Razor-sharp professional order taker. Steppford Marine. They were following an order. Straight, simple.

SAM. And what expert witness are we gonna bring in who's gonna say they had to follow this order?

JO.	KAFFEE.
Jessep.	Kendrick.

JO. (*Pause.*) Jessep.

KAFFEE. I'm not putting Jessep on the stand. I can get what I need from Kendrick.

JO. (*Stands.*) You put Kendrick up there, it gives him a chance to deny he gave the order. Put a Lt. *Colonel* on—

KAFFEE. Dawson and Downey can testify to the order. And Kendrick will testify they had to follow it.

JO. I think that's a mistake.

KAFFEE. Noted.

JO. Thank you.

KAFFEE. Tonight at seven. All I have in the house is Yoo-Hoo and Sugar Smacks. Bring whatever you like to eat and drink, you're gonna be there a while. And don't wear that perfume, it wrecks my concentration.

JO. Really?

KAFFEE. I was talking to Sam.

TOM. Commander Stone to see you, sir.

JESSEP. Thank you, Tom.

(DR, STONE enters. He's tired and he's wearing surgical scrubs.)

JESSEP. Walter, any news?

STONE. Not yet, sir. We've still got a few more tests to run, and they'll take a while. But even at that, I'm not certain we're going to be able to make a determination.

JESSEP. I see.

STONE. Colonel, it would help us to know what happened.

KENDRICK. It was a Code Red, the men were shaving his head.

STONE. Lieutenant, the boy didn't die of a hair cut.

KENDRICK. He died because that's what the Lord saw fit, Commander.

JESSEP. Jesus, Mary and Joseph, Jon, give the Lord a rest, would you please?

KENDRICK. Yes, sir.

JESSEP. *(Pause.)* You look like hell, you get some rest yourself.

(KENDRICK starts to exit, JESSEP stands and stops him.)

JESSEP. Jonny. You're a Marine.

KENDRICK. Thank you, sir. *(Exits.)*

JESSEP. Walter, I don't want to pin you down to anything. I know you've got more tests to run, let me just ask you this: What are the possibilities at this point?

STONE. It could be any number of things, Nathan. They used a gag, it could've gotten stuck in his throat, there could've been something poisonous on the gag, he could've gotten the hell scared out of him and had a heart attack. Like I said, we may never be certain. Sometimes it's a judgment call.

JESSEP. A heart attack?

STONE. He's got a medical history that suggests the possibility of a slight coronary disorder.

JESSEP. Why wasn't this ever detected before?

STONE. It's difficult to impossible to detect in someone that age, and—

JESSEP. Walter, is that what you're gonna say to a board of inquiry?

STONE. How do you mean?

JESSEP. I mean, you give these boys a thorough examination every three months. And every three months you sent Santiago back on that wall with a clean bill of health. Am I wrong?

STONE. Nathan, the symptoms are—

JESSEP. (*Stands.*) Hey, hey, Walter, you tell me. What can happen to a doctor's career because of something like this? (*Pause.*) You know what I think happened? I don't think it was a Code Red. I think Dawson and Downey got it into their heads to kill Santiago. I think, like you said, I think they put poison on the rag.

STONE. That's one possibility.

JESSEP. You know why I think that? Walter, I've know you how many years?

STONE. Four years.

JESSEP. Close on to five now. One of the first things I did when I got this post was request your assignment to the base hospital. And the first thing I'll do when I leave is tell the folks upstairs I want Walter with the big Stones coming with me. I put my trust in you, Walter. I put the lives of my Marines in your hands. That's why I think it had to be poison, Walter. You're the doctor. You're the damn good doctor. Whatever you say, I'll live with it.

(Sits on the table and nods to Stone. STONE's dismissed.)

JESSEP. There's gonna be an investigation into the cause of death. I'll do what I can for you.

STONE. *(Pause.)* Yes, sir. *(Exits.)*

JESSEP. Tom.

TOM. *(Enters.)* Sir.

JESSEP. Find me Captain Markinson.

(LIGHTS out.)

(LIGHTS up on a NAVY ORDERLY standing in front of a table as MARKINSON enters. MARKINSON's wearing civilian clothes and a press pass on his lapel.)

ORDERLY. Yes, can I help you?

MARKINSON. Gosh, I hope so. I've been getting the run-around all morning, Gilbert Hamilton, *Baltimore Sun.*

ORDERLY. What can I do for you?

MARKINSON. I'm doing a two-part feature on the traffic over at Andrews Air Force Base. Do you keep on file any record of incoming flights at Andrews?

ORDERLY. Sure, all the bases. We keep copies of all the daily Tower Chief's Logs.

MARKINSON. Is that right?

ORDERLY. Sure. They list incoming flights, time of arrival, passenger manifests ...

MARKINSON. I need a copy of the log book for Andrews for the evening of July 7th, and the morning of July 8th.

ORDERLY. Got it. The only thing is, I need to see a Fleet requisition form and a 7-10 signed by two officers over the rank of Lieutenant.

MARKINSON. Oh, hell.

ORDERLY. I'm sorry, I can't show copies of the log books without the Fleet requisition form and a 7-10 signed by two officers over the rank of Lieutenant.

MARKINSON. I understand. Is the duty officer here?

ORDERLY. No sir, he's at a department meeting.

MARKINSON. Oh gee, is there anyone else I can speak to?

ORDERLY. Not for another half-hour. Everyone's at lunch. I'm the only one here.

MARKINSON. (*Pulls out a pistol and trains it at the orderly.*) Then let's go and get a log book.

(*LIGHTS up on Brig as KAFFEE enters. DAWSON comes to attention.*)

DAWSON. Sir. Lance Corporal Dawson, sir.

KAFFEE. I know who you are, Harold, you don't have to identify yourself. I thought we were through with this shit the night I struck an enlisted man without cause or provocation.

(*DAWSON says nothing.*)

KAFFEE. I just—I wanted to come by and give you some words of, I don't know, some encouragement or something. (*Reaches into his front left jacket pocket and takes out a large folded piece of paper and reads.*) Sit up straight. (*Folds the paper and puts it back into his pocket.*) Not very confidence inspiring, I know.

DAWSON. It's all right. (*Pause.*) I'm not the one who needs confidence. After all, it's not up to me anymore, is it? (*Pause.*) You have to accept the consequences too. (*Pause.*) Right?

KAFFEE. (*Pause.*) Yeah, but you see, they're not my consequences to accept.

DAWSON. That almost makes it a little bit worse, doesn't it sir?

KAFFEE. (*Long pause as KAFFEE picks up his briefcase and moves to leave.*) Sit up straight.

(*We hear the MARCHING BAND playing in the distance as the LIGHTS come up on the courtroom. The participants begin to enter and move into place, with KAFFEE and ROSS, the last to come in, meeting in the middle of the room.*)

KAFFEE. Last chance. I'll flip you for it.

SERGEANT AT ARMS. Ten-hut.

ROSS. Too late.

(*SERGEANT AT ARMS re-enters followed by JUDGE RANDOLPH.*)

SERGEANT AT ARMS. All those having business with this general court-martial, stand forward and you shall be heard. Captain Julius Alexander Randolph is presiding. God save the United States of America.

JUDGE RANDOLPH. (*Strikes the gavel.*) Without objection, the sworn statements of the defendants have been read to the Members and entered into the court record.

ROSS. No objection.

KAFFEE. No objection.

JUDGE RANDOLPH. Without objection, the sworn statements made by nine members of Rifle Security Company Windward have been read to the jurors and entered into the court record.

ROSS. No objection.

KAFFEE. No objection.

JUDGE RANDOLPH. Is the Government prepared to present its case?

ROSS. We are, sir.

JO. Please the court, before we begin, can I ask if all these MPs are really necessary?

JUDGE RANDOLPH. Are they making you nervous, Commander?

JO. No, sir. They're projecting the image that the defendants are dangerous and/or a flight risk.

ROSS. The defendants are on trial for murder.

JO. The defendants, who are in handcuffs, have not been found guilty of a crime. And I'm certain that if they were to break free and make their escape, the four armed guards at the door would apprehend them.

ROSS. Sir, the Provost Marshal felt it advisable to make the defendants a security priority.

JO. The Provost Marshal is gonna feel like an idiot if someone steals one of our ships during this trial.

JUDGE RANDOLPH. (*Laughs.*) Take your seat, Commander. Government will call its witness.

(*JO sits.*)

ROSS. Government calls Commander Stone.
SERGEANT AT ARMS. Call Commander Stone.

(*COMMANDER STONE enters.*)

ROSS. Commander, have you been previously sworn?
STONE. Yes, I have.

ROSS. Commander, for the record, would you state your full name, rank, and current billet, please.

STONE. Commander Walter Stone. My current billet is internal medicine specialist, Guantanamo Bay Naval Hospital.

ROSS. Thank you, Commander. You may have a seat.

(*STONE sits.*)

ROSS. And you've been attached to the hospital at
GITMO for ...

STONE. From October 1, 1986, to the present.

ROSS. And on 8 July of this year, did you have
occasion to treat Pfc. William Santiago?

STONE. I did.

ROSS. Would you describe that treatment?

STONE. Private Santiago was brought into the
Emergency Room on the morning of the eighth at oh-oh-
thirty. He was coughing up blood and suffering from a lock
of oxygen. He lost consciousness at oh-oh-thirty-five.

ROSS. And what were your observations upon
examination?

STONE. The most obvious things were the rope marks
around his wrists and that his head was partially shaved. X-
rays and lab work revealed this his lungs were filled with
fluid bilaterally. He had profound acidosis. That is to say, a
build-up of acid in his lungs.

ROSS. What causes acid to build up in a person's
lungs?

STONE. Acidosis occurs when the muscles and other
cells of the body burn sugar in the absence of oxygen.
Santiago's cells stopped burning oxygen and began burning
sugar, causing the lungs to bleed. He drowned in his own
blood and was pronounced dead at oh-one-ten.

ROSS. Doctor, what made Santiago's lungs start
burning sugar?

STONE. An ingested poison of some kind.

ROSS. I'm just wondering why it would necessarily
have to be poison. What if, for instance, a rag was placed
in my throat, just as a joke. And maybe the rag was
accidentally pushed too far down, cutting off oxygen
altogether. Wouldn't that trigger the acidosis?

STONE. If that were the case, you'd die of lack of oxygen before your lungs started to bleed. Lactic acidosis is a chemical process that requires twenty to thirty minutes before it becomes lethal.

ROSS. Dr. Stone, did Private Santiago die of poisoning?

STONE. Absolutely.

ROSS. Are you aware that the lab report showed no traces of poison on the rag?

STONE. Yes I am.

ROSS. And are you aware that the coroner's report showed no trace of poison in the body?

STONE. Yes I am.

ROSS. Then how do you justify your opinion, sir?

STONE. There are literally are dozens of toxins which are virtually undetectable, both in a human body and on, well a fabric. The *nature* of the acidosis is the compelling factor in this issue.

ROSS. Thank you, sir.

(*LIGHTS up on Kaffee's apartment. The three LAWYERS are rehearsing cross-examination for the next day.*)

KAFFEE. Doctor, other than the rope marks, was there any external damage?

JO. Don't call him doctor.

KAFFEE. Commander, other than the rope marks, was there any external damage?

SAM. No.

KAFFEE. No scrapes or cuts?

JO. No.

KAFFEE. No bruises or —No—wait—Dammit, why can't I get this?

JO. Concentrate.

KAFFEE. I am concentrating.

JO. Not hard enough.

KAFFEE. I concentrated hard enough to graduate fourth in my class, where's your merit badge for concentration?

JO. Scrapes, cuts, bruises, welts, broken bones, fat-lip.

(*The DOORBELL rings.*)

JO. Saved by the bell.

KAFFEE. Did we order food?

JO. I can't remember.

SAM. I thought we ordered Chinese food.

KAFFEE. We ordered Chinese food yesterday.

SAM. We've ordered Chinese food everyday.

JO. That might be a package for me.

SAM. I'll go. I've gotta stretch my legs. (*Exits.*)

KAFFEE. You're having your mail delivered here now?

JO. I called Division and asked to see the Tower Chief's Log from Guantanamo.

KAFFEE. What do you want with the Tower Chief's Log?

JO. They said the two-hundred was the first flight off the base that night. I want to see if they were keeping Santiago on the base on purpose.

KAFFEE. I'm Chasing Kendrick, you're chasing shadows.

JO. I'm chasing Jessep.

KAFFEE. Keep Jessep out of this.

JO. One day you're gonna tell me what went on in his office.

SAM. (*Returns with a large envelope.*) Well, it's not Chinese food.

JO. Is is for me?

SAM. I don't know. It just says, "AF-40 MAM" M.A.M. Does that mean anything to anybody? (*Turns the envelope over.*)

KAFFEE. AF-40 M.A.M.?

SAM. (*Reading from the other side of the envelope.*)
Lt. Commander Joanne Galloway. USNR, JAGC. M-O-U-S-E.

(*Hands the envelope to Jo, then sits as JO opens the
envelope.*)

KAFFEE. How's the baby?

SAM. I don't know, I haven't see her awake in two
weeks.

JO. (*Taking out a log book from envelope.*) Dammit!

KAFFEE. What?

JO. They sent me the wrong log.

SAM. The wrong week?

JO. The wrong goddamn *base*. They—I swear—these
assholes sent me the Tower Chief's Log from Andrews Air
Force Base. I ask for Naval Air Station, Guantanamo Bay,
Cuba, so naturally they send me Andrews Air Force Base.

SAM. Call 'em in the morning, they'll send you the
right one.

JO. I know, it just galls me.

KAFFEE. It what?

JO. (*Pause.*) It galls me.

KAFFEE. I don't think I've ever heard anyone of my
generation say that before.

JO. Back to work.

KAFFEE. Scrapes, cuts, bruises, welts, broken bones,
fat lip.

JO. Go Harvard.

(*LIGHTS out.*
LIGHTS up on courtroom.
STONE continues on the stand.)

KAFFEE. Commander, you testified that it takes lactic acidosis twenty to thirty minutes before it becomes lethal. That is to say, twenty to thirty minutes before a person's lungs would fill with fluid bilaterally.

STONE. That's correct.

KAFFEE. Twenty to thirty minutes, that's about average.

STONE. Right.

KAFFEE. In some people it might be more, in some people less.

STONE. A little bit more, a little bit less.

KAFFEE. Let me ask you, is it possible for a person to have an affliction, some sort of condition, which might, in the case of this person, actually speed up the process of acidosis dramatically?

STONE. Certainly.

KAFFEE. And what might some of those conditions be?

STONE. If a person had a coronary disorder ... or a cerebral disorder, it's possible that the lungs might begin to bleed before the person suffocated. Mind you, it would have to be a serious condition.

KAFFEE. Is it possible to have a serious coronary condition, where the initial warning signals were so mild as to escape a physician during a routine medical exam?

STONE. Possibly. There would still be symptoms, though.

KAFFEE. And what would some of those symptoms be?

STONE. There are many symptoms of a coronary disorder.

KAFFEE. Are chest pains, shortness of breath and fatigue among them?

STONE. Yes.

KAFFEE. Commander, is this your signature? (*Shows bottom section of document to Stone.*)

STONE. Yes it is.

KAFFEE. This is an order for Private Santiago to be put on restricted duty for a period of four weeks. Would you read your hand written remarks at the bottom of the page, please, sir?

STONE. (*Reading from the document.*) Initial testing negative. Patient complains of chest pains, shortness of breath, fatigue. Restricted from running distances over five and —

KAFFEE. Thank you, Commander, no further questions. (*Goes back to the defense table and sits.*)

ROSS. Doctor Stone, you've held a license to practice medicine for twelve years, you've been published in various medical journals, you are board certified in Internal Medicine, you are the Chief of Internal Medicine at a hospital which serves over 8,000 men. In your professional opinion, Doctor, was Willy Santiago poisoned?

KAFFEE. (*Stands.*) Object. Calls for speculation.

ROSS. Commander Stone is an expert medical witness. In this courtroom his opinion isn't considered speculation.

KAFFEE. Has the witness been admitted as an expert?

ROSS. The Government makes a motion at this time for the court to admit Commander Stone as an expert and to allow his opinion as testimony.

KAFFEE. Defense objects.

JUDGE RANDOLPH. Overruled. The court will hear the doctor's opinion.

KAFFEE. Your Honor, Commander Stone is an internist, not a criminologist, and his testimony under cross-examination has only demonstrated that the medical facts are simply inconclusive.

JUDGE RANDOLPH. Nonetheless, I'd like to hear Dr. Stone's opinion.

(*KAFFEE sits.*)

JO. Sir, the defense strenuously objects and requests a sidebar so that his Honor might have an opportunity to hear discussion before ruling on the objection.

JUDGE RANDOLPH. The objection of the defense has been heard and overruled.

JO. Exception.

JUDGE RANDOLPH. Noted.

(*JO sits.*)

ROSS. Doctor, in your expert, professional opinion, was Willy Santiago poisoned?

STONE. Yes.

ROSS. Thank you, sir. I have no more questions.

JUDGE RANDOLPH. Commander, you may step down.

(*STONE exits.*)

ROSS. Please the court, while the Government reserves its right to call rebuttal witnesses should the need arise, we rest our case. (*Sits.*)

JUDGE RANDOLPH. Is defense ready to present its case?

KAFFEE. Yes, sir.

JUDGE RANDOLPH. Very well. This court will stand in recess until ten hundred hours this Monday, August the 19th. (*Raps gavel.*)

SERGEANT AT ARMS. Ten-hut.

(*ALL stand. JUDGE exits.*)

SERGEANT AT ARMS. Dismissed.

(*The courtroom begins clearing out. The DEFENDANTS are led off by MPs; ROSS follows.*)

SAM. I strenuously object? Is that how it works? Objection. Overruled. No, no, no, no I strenuously object. Well, if you strenuously object, let me take a moment to reconsider.

JO. Look, I got it in the record.

SAM. You also got it in the jury's head we're afraid of the doctor. You object once to remind them his testimony hasn't been proven, but any more than that, and it looks like this great case we built was just a lot of fancy lawyer tricks. It's just the difference between paper law and trial—

(*KAFFEE puts his hand on Sam's arm to stop him.*)

SAM. I'm sorry, I'm in a pissy mood.

JO. (*Takes a moment; then to Kaffee.*) Is he right?

SAM. *Yes* I'm right.

KAFFEE. Yes he's right, but—

JO. Okay.

KAFFEE. He's right. But it doesn't matter.

(*There's an uncomfortable silence. SAM crosses up the steps.*)

SAM. I'm gonna go call my wife. I'll meet you later.

(*SAM starts to exit.*)

JO. Why do you hate them so much?

(*This stops SAM in his tracks.*)

SAM. They beat up on a weakling, and that's all they did. The rest is smoke-filled, coffee-house crap. They tortured and tormented a weaker kid. And it wasn't just that night, read the letters, it was eight months. And you know what? I'll bet it was his whole life. They beat him up, and they killed him. And why? Because he couldn't run very fast. I'm off duty now, don't ask me to be pals with these guys.

JO. Sam, do you think the argument we're going to make on Monday is legally sound?

SAM. I think the argument we're going to make on Monday is morally reprehensible.

KAFFEE. I'm not a judge, Sam. I'm not a jury, and I'm not a prosecutor. That makes me the on person in the room who is *honor bound* to do things which are morally reprehensible. (*A long silence. KAFFEE stands and puts his case on the table.*) All right, everybody take the night off.

SAM. Danny, I—

KAFFEE. I mean it. Go see Laura, see your daughter. Jo, do whatever it is you do when you're not here. We'll start working on Howard tomorrow. (*Pause.*)

SAM. Shouldn't we—

KAFFEE. No. (*Pause.*) Take the night off. (*Pause.*)

SAM. I'll see you in the morning. (*Exits.*)

KAFFEE. (*Picks case up off table.*) He's tired. He'll be fine. I'll see you tomorrow.

JO. How much damage did I cause. With the doctor?

KAFFEE. It doesn't matter.

JO. Are you saying it doesn't matter 'cause I didn't cause that much damage, or doesn't matter 'cause it's water under the bridge?

KAFFEE. It doesn't matter 'cause we'll never know and and there's nothing we can do about it.

JO. Good. That's a good attitude.

KAFFEE. Thank you. I got it on sale. I'll see you in the morning. (*Starts to leave, stops and turns toward Jo.*) Jo, do you have anyplace to go?

JO. Yeah I was just gonna stick around here a little while.

KAFFEE. Here in the courtroom?

JO. Yeah.

KAFFEE. (*Pause.*) The only person around here is gonna be Dickey the night janitor, and he's asleep most of the time. Quite honestly he's not that much fun when he's awake.

JO. I know I just ...

KAFFEE. What?

JO. Nothing.

KAFFEE. What?

JO. Nothing.

KAFFEE. You just what?

JO. I enjoy empty courtrooms.

KAFFEE. You enjoy empty courtrooms.

JO. Yes.

KAFFEE. You're like seven of the strangest women I've ever met.

JO. I know. I'm the girl guys like you hated in sixth grade.

KAFFEE. Jo, you're the girl guys like me tortured in sixth grade. I'll see you tomorrow. (*Pause.*) Why do you like them so much?

JO. 'Cause they stand on a wall. (*Pause.*) And they say nothing's gonna hurt you tonight. (*Pause.*) Not on my watch. (*Pause.*) Isn't that amazing?

KAFFEE. Don't worry about the doctor. This trial starts Monday.

(*LIGHTS up on Markinson wearing full dress uniform.*)

MARKINSON. Dear Mr. and Mrs. Santiago. I was William's Company Commander. I knew your son vaguely, which is to say I knew his name. In a matter of time, the trial of the two men charged with your son's death will be concluded, and seven men and two women whom you've never met will try and offer you an explanation as to why William is dead. Most likely, they will offer many explanations. For my part, I've done what I can to bring the truth to light. I've done it, not in the uniform in which I served for twenty-one years, but in costumes and in shadows. I was a defender. And at this moment I'm being pursued by the Naval Investigative Service, the Federal Bureau of Investigations, the Central Intelligence Agency and the Military Police. And I can't possibly do this anymore. Because the truth is this: Your son is dead for only one reason. I wasn't strong enough to stop it. Always, Captain Matthew Andrew Markinson, United States Marine Corps.

(MARKINSON waits a moment before he takes out a pistol, cocks it, sticks it in his mouth, and pulls trigger.
The LIGHTS go to black as we hear the sound of a GUNSHOT.
We hear the MARINES CHANTING.)

MARINES. *(Chanting.)*
I WANT TO BE A RECON RANGER
I want to be a Recon Ranger
I WANT TO LIVE A LIFE OF DANGER
I want to live a life of danger
STAND TALL
Do it again
SING IT LOUD

Three Four
LEFT RIGHT
One Two Three Four
One Two—
—Stand proud!

(*Courtroom.*)

SERGEANT AT ARMS. Ten-hut.

(*JUDGE RANDOLPH strikes the gavel.*)

SERGEANT AT ARMS. Today is Monday, 19 August, 86. Session is called to order at ten hundred and two.

(*KAFFEE enters late and takes his place at the defense table.*)

SAM. Where've you been?
KAFFEE. Stop looking for Markinson.
JUDGE RANDOLPH. Is defense ready to call its first witness?
KAFFEE. Yes sir. Defense calls Corporal Howard.
SERGEANT AT ARMS. Call Corporal Howard.

(*HOWARD enters.*)

ROSS. Corporal Howard, have you previously been sworn in?
HOWARD. Yes, sir.
ROSS. Corporal, would you state your full name, rank and current billet for the record, please?
HOWARD. Corporal Jeffrey Owen Howard, Marine Barracks Windward, Guantanamo Bay, Cuba.

ROSS. Thank you Corporal. You may have a seat.

(*HOWARD sits in witness chair.*)

KAFFEE. Corporal, are you a little nervous?
HOWARD. Yes, sir.
KAFFEE. Would you like a glass of water?
HOWARD. No sir, I'm fine thank you.
KAFFEE. You sure?
HOWARD. Yes, sir.
KAFFEE. Well if you want some water or if you'd like to have a short break, you just let me know.
ROSS. Please the court, the witness has twice said he doesn't want any water, can we proceed with the examination?
JUDGE RANDOLPH. Defense counsel will question the witness.
KAFFEE. Corporal, you've been called as a witness in order to give the court some insight into the nature of the duty that the Marines in Rifle Security Company perform. Please feel free to use the map that's behind you.
HOWARD. Well ... it's very simple really. The base is divided into two halves—
KAFFEE. Corporal, you're gonna have to wait for me to ask a question.
HOWARD. Yes sir. I'm sorry, sir.
KAFFEE. (*Pause.*) Would you describe the general layout of the base for us?
HOWARD. Yes sir. It's very simple really. The base is divided into two halves, the divider being Guantanamo Bay. Each half of the base has its own Rifle Security Company. On the left side is RSC Leeward, see, and the right side is Windward.
KAFFEE. What's the function of the Marines in RSC Windward?

HOWARD. To provide ground support in the event of an enemy engagement and to provide day-to-day security on the fenceline.

KAFFEE. How much time do the Marines spend on watch?

HOWARD. We're on the fence for one week, then off for a week.

KAFFEE. And when you're on the fence, how long is each watch?

HOWARD. Six hours on, six hours off.

KAFFEE. Six hours on, six hours off, one week on, one week off, is that right?

HOWARD. Yes sir.

KAFFEE. Are the sentries armed?

HOWARD. Yes sir.

KAFFEE. With ...?

HOWARD. Sir?

KAFFEE. What are the Marines armed with?

HOWARD. Sir?

KAFFEE. What are you armed, with, Jeffrey?

HOWARD. Weapons.

KAFFEE. A pea shooter, a pocket knife, a sling-shot?

HOWARD. Oh, no, sir. (*Laughs to himself.*) A pea shooter.

KAFFEE. Permission to lead the witness?

JUDGE RANDOLPH. By a leash, if necessary.

KAFFEE. You're armed with M-15 rifles and 60 rounds of ammunition, is that right?

HOWARD. Yes, sir.

KAFFEE. Okay. Jeffrey, what's a Code Red?

HOWARD. Sir, a Code Red is a disciplinary action brought against a Marine who's fallen out of line.

KAFFEE. Name some ways a Marine could fall out of line.

HOWARD. Being late for Platoon or Company meetings, keeping his barracks in disorder, letting his personal appearance become sub-standard, behaving in a manner unbecoming a Marine, falling back on a run ...

KAFFEE. Have you ever received a Code Red?

HOWARD. Yes, sir.

KAFFEE. Would you describe it.

HOWARD. I dropped my weapon during a field exercise one day. We were doing seven-man assault drills and I dropped my weapon. It's just that my palms were sweaty 'cause it was over a hundred degrees and my weapon just slipped, sir.

KAFFEE. And what happened?

HOWARD. Well that night in my barracks the guys in my squad threw a blanket over me and took turns punching me in the arm for five minutes. Then they poured glue on my hands.

KAFFEE. Okay—

HOWARD. It worked, too, 'cause I ain't never dropped my weapon since.

ROSS. Object.

KAFFEE. We're gonna have to strike that, Jeffrey, but it was a good effort. What happened after they punched you and poured glue on your hands?

HOWARD. They took me to the Post 44 and bought me a beer.

KAFFEE. They gave you a Code Red, then they bought you a beer.

HOWARD. Yes, sir.

KAFFEE. Corporal, were you acquainted with Private Santiago?

HOWARD. Yes, sir.

KAFFEE. Did you come in contact with him every day?

HOWARD. Yes, sir.

KAFFEE. You participated in drills together?

HOWARD. Yes, sir.

KAFFEE. Your squads were on the fence together?

HOWARD. Yes, sir.

KAFFEE. You shared a barracks hall?

HOWARD. Yes, sir.

KAFFEE. Was Private Santiago ever late for platoon meetings?

HOWARD. Yes, sir.

KAFFEE. Was his barracks ever in disorder?

HOWARD. Yes, sir.

KAFFEE. Did he ever let his appearance become substandard?

HOWARD. Yes, sir.

KAFFEE. Did he ever fall back on a run?

HOWARD. All the time, sir.

KAFFEE. Did he ever, in your estimation, behave in a manner unbecoming a Marine?

HOWARD. Absolutely, sir, yes.

KAFFEE. Did he ever, prior to the morning of July 8th, receive a Code Red?

HOWARD. No, sir.

KAFFEE. (*Pause*.) Never? You got a Code Red 'cause your palms were sweaty, why didn't Private Santiago, this burden and embarrassment to his unit, why didn't he ever get a Code Red?

HOWARD. Corporal Dawson wouldn't allow it, sir.

KAFFEE. Corporal Dawson wouldn't allow it.

HOWARD. Hal—Corporal Dawson, was Santiago's squad leader. He wouldn't allow anyone to go near him, sir. The guys talked tough about Santiago but when it came down to it they wouldn't touch him. The were too afraid of Corporal Dawson, sir.

ROSS. Object. The witness is characterizing.

KAFFEE. Good point. I'll rephrase. Jeffrey, did you ever want to give Santiago a Code Red?

HOWARD. Yes, sir.

KAFFEE. Why didn't you?

HOWARD. 'Cause Dawson'd kick my butt, sir.

KAFFEE. Good enough. Lt. Ross is gonna ask you some questions now.

(KAFFEE sits at the defense table. ROSS stands, opens his case, takes out three books, keeps one in his hand and puts the other two down on the table as HE crosses to Howard.)

ROSS. Corporal, I hold here *The Marine Guide and General Information Handbook for New Recruits.* Are you familiar with this book?

HOWARD. Yes, sir.

ROSS. Have you read it?

HOWARD. Yes, sir.

ROSS. Good. *(Hands him the book.)* Would you turn to the chapter that deals with Code Reds, please.

HOWARD. Sir?

ROSS. Just flip to the page in that book that discusses Code Reds.

HOWARD. Code Reds aren't in this book, sir.

ROSS. I see. *(Goes back to his table and gets another book.)* Let's turn then to the *Marine Infantry Handbook.* Would you find us the section on Code Reds in this book and read it to us please?

HOWARD. Sir, you see, Code Red is a Marine term that—we only use it down at GITMO, sir. I don't know if it actually—

ROSS. We're in luck then. *(Gets the third book.)* *The Marine Corps Guide for Sentry Duty, NAVBASE Guantanamo Bay, Cuba.* I assume we'll find the term Code

Red and its definition in this book, and then we can move on, am I correct, Corporal?

HOWARD. No, sir.

ROSS. No? Corporal Howard, I'm a Marine. Is there no book, no manual, or pamphlet, no set of orders or regulations that let me know that, as a Marine, one of my duties is to perform Code Reds?

HOWARD. (*Pause.*) No sir. No books, sir.

ROSS. No further questions.

(KAFFEE gets one of the books from Ross's table.)

KAFFEE. Corporal, would you turn to the page in this book that says where the Enlisted Men's Mess Hall is?

HOWARD. Lt. Kaffee, that's not in the book.

KAFFEE. No? You mean to tell the court that you've been stationed in GITMO for thirteen months and in all that time you've never had a meal?

HOWARD. No, sir. Three squares a day.

KAFFEE. I'm confused. How did you know where the mess hall was if it's not in this book?

HOWARD. I guess I just followed the crowd at chow time, sir.

KAFFEE. No more questions.

JUDGE RANDOLPH. You can step down, Corporal Howard.

HOWARD. Thank you, sir.

JUDGE RANDOLPH. We'll take a five minute recess. Please don't anybody go too far. (*Raps the gavel.*)

SERGEANT AT ARMS. Ten-hut.

(EVERYONE stands. The JUDGE exits .)

SERGEANT AT ARMS. As you were.

SAM. What happened to Markinson?

(*KAFFEE whispers briefly to Sam and Jo.*)

JO. Christ.

ROSS. (*Walks up to Kaffee.*) Can I talk to you alone for a minute?

(*KAFFEE and ROSS move off to the side.*

ROSS. That was nice work. The re-direct on Howard.

KAFFEE. Thank you.

ROSS. I want this to end now. I don't want Kendrick to have to take the stand.

KAFFEE. He's a real day at the beach, isn't he?

ROSS. I was up half the night with him. He's bright, articulate, nothing in the closet, and you're gonna make a meal out of him.

KAFFEE. What're you getting at, Jack?

ROSS. That's what I wanted to ask you. You're putting on an entertaining defense that's going nowhere. You had the doctor on the ropes—

KAFFEE. I'm done talking to—

ROSS. Listen to me. You had the doctor on the ropes and you lost him, you know you did. Howard was sweet as hell with his Dawson the protector number and now you're gonna trash Kendrick to make it look like you're doing your job, when you and I know, and don't pretend you don't, that it doesn't get you one step closer to where you need to be.

KAFFEE. We've got two minutes to the Reverend Jon, what can I do for you?

ROSS. Don't put Kendrick on the stand. I have to protect these guys. I can't allow them to look like clowns up there. Stop now. Three years apiece.

KAFFEE. Are you joking? Four weeks ago we were talking about six months.

ROSS. Four weeks ago your clients pissed on six months. Four weeks ago your clients weren't a daily feature in the Washington *Post*, and neither were you. You've only go two witnesses, and they're both suspected of murder.

KAFFEE. (*Turning to leave.*) Thanks Jack.

ROSS. (*Raising his voice.*) You got bullied into this room. By everybody. By her, by Dawson. I mean, I practically dared you. You got bullied into this room, even though not for a second have you believed you could win. You got bullied into this room by the memory of a lawyer who might've stood a chance.

KAFFEE. You're a lousy, fuckin' softball player, Jack.

SERGEANT AT ARMS. Ten-hut.

(*JUDGE RANDOLPH enters.*)

ROSS. Your boys are going down and I can't stop it anymore.

(*ROSS crosses back to his seat. JUDGE RANDOLPH raps the gavel.*)

KAFFEE. Defense calls Lt. Jonathan James Kendrick.

SERGEANT AT ARMS. Call Lt. Kendrick.

(*KENDRICK enters.*)

ROSS. Lieutenant Kendrick, have you been previously sworn in?

KENDRICK. I have.

ROSS. Would you state your full name, rank, and current billet for the record, please?

KENDRICK. Lieutenant Jonathan James Kendrick, Executive Officer, Rifle Security Company Windward, NAVBASE Guantanamo Bay.

ROSS. Thank you, Lieutenant. You can have a seat.

KAFFEE. Lt. Kendrick, in your opinion was Private Santiago a good Marine?

KENDRICK. I'd say he was about average.

KAFFEE. (*Getting some documents from Jo.*) Lieutenant, you co-signed three fitness reports on Santiago. On all three reports you indicated a rating of Below Average.

KENDRICK. Yes. Private Santiago was Below Average. I didn't see the need to trample on a man's grave.

KAFFEE. (*Puts folder down on table.*) We appreciate that, but you're under oath now, and I think, unpleasant as it may be, we'd all just as soon hear the truth.

KENDRICK. I'm aware of my oath.

KAFFEE. On your left bicep is a patch. Would you tell us what that patch says?

KENDRICK. Unit. Corps. God. Country.

KAFFEE. And what does that slogan mean?

KENDRICK. It's our order of priorities. It's our Code.

KAFFEE. Would Private Santiago be as likely to adhere to that Code as someone who received a rating of Exceptional?

KENDRICK. No, he would not.

(*KAFFEE gets another file.*)

KAFFEE. Lieutenant, these are the last three fitness reports you signed for Lance Corporal Dawson and Pfc. Downey. Private Downey received three straight marks of Exceptional. Lance Corporal Dawson received two marks of Exceptional, but on the most recent report, dated June 9th of this year, he was given an overall rating of Below

Average. It's this last report that I'd like to discuss for a moment, sir.

KENDRICK. That's fine.

KAFFEE. Lance Corporal Dawson's ranking after Infantry Training School was 4 point zero. Records indicate that well over half that class has since been promoted to full Corporal, while Dawson has remained a Lance Corporal. Was Dawson's promotion held up because of this last fitness report?

KENDRICK. I'm sure it was.

KAFFEE. Lieutenant, do you recall why Dawson was given such a poor grade on this report?

KENDRICK. I'm sure I don't. I have many men in my charge, Lieutenant. I write many fitness reports.

KAFFEE. Do you recall an incident involving a Pfc. Curtis Barnes who'd been found stealing liquor from the Officer's Club?

KENDRICK. Yes I do, as a matter of fact. I recall thinking very highly of Private Barnes and not wanting to see his record tarnished by a formal charge.

KAFFEE. You preferred instead to handle it within the unit.

ROSS. Object.

KAFFEE. I remind the court that Lieutenant Kendrick is appearing as an adverse witness and that the rules of cross and not direct examination apply.

JUDGE RANDOLPH. Overruled.

KAFFEE. Any real leader will tell you that the best way to handle a low level problem is to let those on a low level handle it.

KAFFEE. Lieutenant, did you order Corporal Dawson and two other men to make sure that Private Barnes receive no food or drink except water for a period of ten days?

KENDRICK. That is a distortion of the truth. Private Barnes was placed on barracks restriction. He was given water and vitamin supplements. I assure you that at no time was his health in danger.

ROSS. Please the court, the Government objects to this entire line of questioning as argumentative and irrelevant badgering of the witness.

JUDGE RANDOLPH. Lieutenant, I remind you that you are now questioning a Marine officer with an impeccable service record.

ROSS. Thank you, Judge.

JUDGE RANDOLPH. You're welcome. (*Pause.*) I'm overruling your objection. Defense may continue its line of questioning.

KAFFEE. Lieutenant, you said that you prefer to handle these situations within the unit, rather than going through what this court might consider to be proper authorities. Is that right?

KENDRICK. I beg your pardon?

KAFFEE. Would you like me to repeat the question?

KENDRICK. Proper authorities?

KAFFEE. Yes.

KENDRICK. I have two books at my bedside, Lieutenant. The Marine Code of Conduct and the King James Bible. The only proper authorities I'm aware of are my commanding Officer Colonel Nathan Roy Jessep and the Lord our God.

KAFFEE. Lieutenant, at your request, I can ask that the record reflect your lack of recognition of this court as a proper authority.

ROSS. Move to strike.

JUDGE RANDOLPH. Counsel, I'd advise against testing the limits of my practice.

KAFFEE. Yes, sir. (*To Kendrick.*) Lieutenant, the sort of disciplinary action you preferred in the matter of Curtis Barnes, is there a name for it?

ROSS. (*Stands.*) Object—

KENDRICK. It's called Code Red and it works and it's the business of no one but the members of Rifle Security Company.

KAFFEE. Well, we've got that straightened out anyway.

KENDRICK. Well, I certainly hope so.

KAFFEE. Would a Marine with an overall rating of Exceptional know what a Code Red is?

KENDRICK. Yes, he sure would.

KAFFEE. Now let me ask you this, Lieutenant, was Lance Corporal Dawson given a rating of Below Average because you learned he was sneaking food to Private Barnes?

KENDRICK. (*Pause.*) Lance Corporal Dawson was found to be Below Average because he committed a crime.

KAFFEE. What crime did he commit?

KENDRICK. He disobe— (*Pause.*)

KAFFEE. Lieutenant Kendrick, what crime did Dawson commit? (*Pause.*)

KENDRICK. He disobeyed an order.

KAFFEE. He disobeyed an order that you gave for Private Barnes to receive a Code Red.

KENDRICK. Yes.

KAFFEE. And because he did, because he exercised his conscience, because he made a decision, he was punished, is that right? (*Pause.*) Lieutenant?

KENDRICK. No, because he disobeyed an order.

KAFFEE. Yeah, but it wasn't a real order, was it? After all, it's peace time. He wasn't being asked to secure a hill ... or radio for Battalion Aid ... or advance on a beachhead. I mean, surely a Marine with Dawson's outstanding service record can be trusted to determine on his *own* which orders are the really important orders, and which orders might, say, be illegal.

KENDRICK. No. No, it wasn't Corporal Dawson's prerogative.

KAFFEE. A lesson he learned after the Curtis Barnes incident, am I right?

KENDRICK. I would think so.

KAFFEE. You know so, don't you Lieutenant?

ROSS. (*Stands.*) Object.

KAFFEE. Withdrawn. No more questions.

ROSS. Did you have a meeting with the members of Second Platoon on the evening of 7 July?

KENDRICK. Yes, I did.

ROSS. And what did you tell them, Lieutenant?

KENDRICK. That Private Santiago was being transferred off the base at oh two hundred. And that he was not to be touched.

ROSS. Thank you, Lt. Kendrick.

(*LIGHTS up on Kaffee's apartment.*)

JO. (*With a deli bag.*) Coffee.

KAFFEE. We got the Tower Chief's log from Guantanamo.

JO. And?

KAFFEE. Nothing. The first plane off the base was at two that morning, the flight Jessep booked him on.

JO. Damn.

KAFFEE. We're okay. We did a job on Kendrick.

JO. I wanted Jessep.

KAFFEE. Jessep's not our job. The order came from Kendrick. The cover-up's not our job. Someone else'll go after Jessep.

JO. Nobody's gonna go after Jessep.

KAFFEE. Dawson and Downey, Jo. We work for Dawson and Downey.

JO. Right ... Right ... All right ... Okay. You remember the order of the questions?

KAFFEE. Yes.

JO. Are you sure?

KAFFEE. Yes.

JO. You'll use small words?

KAFFEE. Yes.

JO. He gets rattled when he doesn't understand something.

KAFFEE. We're all set all right?

JO. When he doesn't understand something, he thinks he's in trouble.

KAFFEE. Jo—

JO. I'm just saying, go slow.

KAFFEE. I'm gonna go slow.

JO. Okay.

KAFFEE. All right.

JO. And get him off as fast as you can.

KAFFEE. Joanne—

JO. All right.

KAFFEE. Okay. (*Pause.*) I think we might win. (*Pause.*) If Downey comes through. And then Dawson. (*Pause.*) I think we might win.

JO. We are. We're gonna win. (*Pause.*) Be sure and make a lot of eye contract, so that—

(*KAFFEE has been playing with the baseball bat throughout. HE pretends to swing at Jo.*)

JO. Right. You want some coffee?

KAFFEE. Yes, please. You can't have any, though.

JO. Hey, I'm just psyched, brother, I'm juiced

KAFFEE. You're wired.

JO. Sam, you want some coffee?

SAM. I'll take a Yoo-Hoo.

JO. You're gonna have a Yoo-Hoo?

SAM. (*Pause*.) Yeah.

JO. Okay.

SAM. (*Pause*.) I want a Yoo-Hoo, is that such a big deal? He asks for a Yoo-Hoo and it's like he's asking for the correct time. I ask for a Yoo-Hoo and the world is coming to an end. I'm gonna get myself a Yoo-Hoo, okay? Can we drop it now? I want a Yoo-Hoo.

KAFFEE. Sam.

SAM. I'm fine. (*Pause*.) I think we're gonna win.

(*LIGHTS up on courtroom.*)

DOWNEY. (*On the stand*.) We were taken into custody by the military police officers and taken to the brig.

KAFFEE. Private Downey, this is my last question for you. Why did you give Pfc. Santiago a Code Red on the evening of July 7th?

DOWNEY. The Code Red was ordered by the Executive Officer, sir, Lt. Kendrick.

KAFFEE. Thank you very much.

ROSS. Private, for the week of 2 July, the switch log has you at Post 39, is that correct?

DOWNEY. I'm sure it is, sir. They keep that log pretty good.

ROSS. How far is Post 39 from Windward barracks?

DOWNEY. It's a ways, sir, it's a hike.

ROSS. About how far by jeep? How many minutes would you say?

DOWNEY. About 15, 20 minutes by jeep, sir.

ROSS. Have you ever had to walk it?

DOWNEY. Yes, sir. That week, sir, Friday. I was DDL. The Pick-up Private—sir, that's what we call the fella who drops us at our post and picks us up, also 'cause he can get girls in New York City—

DOWNEY. —the Pick-up Private got a flat. Right at 39. He pulled up and blam, a blow-out with no spare, sir. The two us us had to double-time it back to the barracks.

ROSS. And if it's 15 or 20 minutes by jeep, I'm guessing it must be a good hour by foot, am I close?

DOWNEY. Me and Pick-up did it in 45 flat, sir.

ROSS. Not bad. And you say your assault on Willy Santiago was the result of an order that Lt. Kendrick gave at a platoon meeting at sixteen-twenty hours?

(*Pause.*)

DOWNEY. Sir?

ROSS. You testified that this meeting where Lt. Kendrick gave you an order to perform a Code Red took place at sixteen-twenty, twenty minutes after your squad was relieved on the fence that evening. But you just said that you didn't make it back to Windward barracks until sixteen forty-five. (*Pause.*)

DOWNEY. No, you see, sir, there was a flat tire.

ROSS. Private, were you at the meeting?

DOWNEY. Sir?

ROSS. (*Pause.*) Were you at the meting that Lieutenant Kendrick held with the members of Second Platoon, Delta?

DOWNEY. (*Pause.*) No, sir. You see, there was a flat tire.

ROSS. (*Crossing toward Downey.*) You never heard Lt. Kendrick say "Give Santiago a Code Red." (*Pause.*) Did Corporal Dawson order you to give Santiago a Code Red?

SAM. (*Standing.*) Objection.

JO. (*Standing.*) Please the court, I'd like to request a recess to confer with my client.

ROSS. I'd like an answer to my question.

JO. The witness has *rights*—

ROSS. The witness has been *read* his rights, Commander.

DOWNEY. (*To Jo.*) Ma'am—?

JUDGE RANDOLPH. The question will be repeated.

DOWNEY. Ma'am—?

ROSS. Did Corporal Dawson order you to give Willy Santiago a Code Red?

DOWNEY. We had—(*Pause.*) Sir, I didn't—(*Pause.*)

JUDGE RANDOLPH. Direct your client to answer the question.

DOWNEY.—We did it in forty-five flat, sir.

JO. (*Standing.*) You must grant the defense a recess.

JUDGE RANDOLPH. Lt. Kaffee, please direct your client to answer the question.

JO. Private Downey is *my* client, and I am addressing the court—

DOWNEY. It was a Code Red—

JUDGE RANDOLPH. Lieutenant, please handle your client!

DAWSON. (*Stands.*) *HEP!*

(*Pause.*)

DAWSON. Private. Answer the Lieutenant's question.

(*The room is silent from DAWSON's outburst. But then DOWNEY does the most amazing thing. HE transforms before our eyes. HE sits up straight and tall, screws up his courage in a manner we've only seen from Dawson, and speaks with all the pride there is.*)

DOWNEY. Yes, Lieutenant. I was given an order. By my Squad Leader, Lance Corporal Harold W. Dawson of the U.S. Marine Corps. And I followed it.

(*BLACKOUT.*)

MARINES. (*Chanting.*)
WHAT ARE YOU GONNA DO WHEN YOU GET
   BACK?
What are you gonna do when you get back?
TAKE A SHOWER AND HIT THE RACK.
Take a shower and hit the rack.
OH NO
Not me
OH NO
Not us
What are we gonna do when we get back?
Polish up for a sneak attack

(*LIGHTS up on Kaffee's apartment.*
SAM and JO sit silently. A few packing cartons lay about.
   After a long moment, KAFFEE walks in with his
   briefcase. He seems remarkably calm.)

SAM. Danny, what'd he say?
KAFFEE. (*Removes some papers and files from his*
case and places them in the box.) He'll give Downey
Involuntary. He'll do seven years. Dawson'll have to plead
guilty to the higher court. Twelve to fifteen. He wants an
answer tonight. (*Stops packing. Picks up the box and*
looks at JO, who seems to be expecting something more.)
What do you want me to say? That no lawyer in the world
would've thought to check out something like that? ... I
would've. He would've.
JO. Then why didn't you?
KAFFEE. (*Finally explodes. Throws the box to the*
floor.) Because I trusted you! Two guys who were about to
do six months are going away for two decades between
them. Because I trusted you. But that was today: that was

before I talked to Ross. Did you tell Aunt Ginny about
your track record? Did you tell her that you've gone into
court six times in your life, and that you lost each time?
Your passion is compelling, Jo. It's also useless because
Louden Downey needed a trial lawyer today. (*Calmly, HE
starts cleaning up papers and file folders off the floor,
putting them back into the box.*) Anyway. that's that.

JO. (*Shaken. SHE picks up her case and stands.*) I still
think we can win. I think you're using what happened
today as an excuse to give up. I think you're afraid of
Jessep, Danny, and I think you're just destined to be a
victim of your own fear. But what the hell you still get the
steak knives.

KAFFEE. Get the fuck out.

(*JO exits. Long pause.
KAFFEE stands there a moment before picking up the box
and throwing it again to the floor, then crosses up the
steps knocking his brief case SR off the platform/out of
his way as HE exits.
SAM stands, crosses to the box, kneels and begins picking
things up off the floor and replaces them in the box.
KAFFEE returns seconds later drinking from a bottle as:*)

KAFFEE. Stop cleaning up.

(*SAM continues to pick the papers up off the floor and to
make some attempt to organize the mess.*)

KAFFEE. Sam. Stop cleaning up.

(*SAM stops and looks at Kaffee.*)

KAFFEE. Do you think if we'd been able to find
Markinson it would've made a difference?

SAM. No. I don't know. Who knows what Markinson knew? Maybe he was just a coward with a conscience.

KAFFEE. (*Pause. Offering bottle of whisky to Sam.*) You want a drink?

SAM. Yeah.

KAFFEE. (*Pause.*) Is your father proud of you?

SAM. Don't do this to yourself.

KAFFEE. Is he? Is he very proud of you?

SAM. Sure.

KAFFEE. I'll bet he is. I'll bet your dad bores the shit out of the neighbors, guys he works with, aunts, uncles ... "Sam made Law Review ... Sam—Sam's got a big case he's making—he's arguing—he's making an argument (*Pause.*) I think my father would have enjoyed seeing me graduate from law school. I think he would have liked that ... an awful lot. (*Pause.*) I'm very angry about that, Sam.

SAM. I know you are.

KAFFEE. I have to call Ross. I said I'd call him at home before midnight.

SAM. I'll call him. Do you have the number?

KAFFEE. In my book. In my briefcase.

(*SAM stands, picks up Kaffee's briefcase.*)

SAM. (*Scratching his thumb on the security tag.*) Ow shit!

KAFFEE. What?

SAM. I cut myself on your damn security tag.

KAFFEE. God. I never took it off. (*Removes the tag, puts the case down on the floor, then examines the security tag that he had put on his briefcase at GITMO. HE stops for a moment.*)

SAM. If you give me Ross's number. I'll call him. (*Pause.*) Danny.

KAFFEE. (*Quietly.*) It galls me.

SAM. What?

KAFFEE. (*To himself.*) It galls me.

SAM. I can't hear you.

KAFFEE. It galls me.

SAM. Yeah. We need to call Ross.

KAFFEE. Call him. Tell him thanks a lot, but no deal. Tell him I'm requesting a 24-hour continuance to subpoena Colonel Jessep.

SAM. What?

KAFFEE. I've been going after the wrong guy.

SAM. What're you talking about?

KAFFEE. Do you remember when we flew back from Cuba?

SAM. It was around six.

KAFFEE. Do you remember our flight code?

SAM. Why would I remember—

KAFFEE. AF-40. Doesn't have any windows, but it flies.

SAM. Yeah I remember that but—

KAFFEE. Do you remember the wrong log book they sent Jo? The one that galled her? The Tower Chief's Log from Andrews?

SAM. AF-40. AF-40 *MAM*.

KAFFEE. *MAM* Matthew A. Markinson. Coward with a conscience. Why it took me five weeks to figure it out is beyond me. But given time I'll think of a way to blame it on you. (*Stands, crosses to box.*) Let's go, you gotta prep me for Jessep and I need Jo to write the motion for the continuance.

SAM. Look. Wait. Let's just siddown with Ross. If Jessep tampered with evidence, we might be able to get a new deal.

KAFFEE. I don't want Jessep on evidence tampering. I want him to say he ordered the Code Red. Let's go.

SAM. You still need a witness.

KAFFEE. I have a witness.

SAM. A dead witness.

KAFFEE. And in the hands of a lesser attorney, that would be a problem.

SAM. You're gonna trip Jessep.

KAFFEE. I'm not gonna trip him. I'm gonna lead him right where he's dying to go.

SAM. I don't think you can do it.

KAFFEE. I know you don't. Let's go.

SAM. Doesn't that mean anything to you?

KAFFEE. A great deal. But let me ask you this. What if I'm twice as good as you think I am? What if I'm not some half-assed clown of a Phi Beta Kappa used car salesman?

SAM. You'd still need a window. He has no weakness. He won't let you near him.

KAFFEE. He has a weakness.

SAM. What?!

KAFFEE. He thinks he was right. Let's go.

SAM. You shoot at Jessep and miss, Randolph'll cite you—listen to me—Randolph'll cite you for contempt. If they decide to teach you a lesson, they'll slap you with a dishonorable discharge and that'll be stapled to every job application you ever fill out.

KAFFEE. Life's like that sometimes. Let's go.

SAM. You're that sure.

KAFFEE. Yeah.

SAM. He's gonna confess.

KAFFEE. Yeah. You know why?

SAM. No.

KAFFEE. Because he has honor. And he has a Code. And I'm twice as good as you think I am. Let's go.

(*BLACKOUT*.)

(LIGHTS up on the courtroom. It's empty and dark except for JO sitting in the witness chair, very much lost in thought.
We hear KAFFEE and SAM as they walk in slowly.)

KAFFEE. Say, Sam? Have you ever heard the story of the Lt. Commander and the Lt. Colonel?

SAM. I believe I have, Danny. It's a story of courage and conviction, is it not?

KAFFEE. Right you are, Sam. You see, the Lt. Commander was investigating a crime and she had a question she wanted the Colonel to answer.

SAM. This Colonel is a very intimidating character, I've heard.

KAFFEE. Well, sure, to some people. To some people he's the stuff of which nightmares are made.

SAM. But not to Commander Galloway.

KAFFEE. No, sir. 'Cause Commander Galloway ain't scared a nothin'. She had a question. And she was gonna get an answer. *(Pause.)* And she was confident. And she was relentless. *(Drops the routine and speaks directly to Jo.)* And she did her job.

JO. What do you want?

KAFFEE. I want to talk to you about Lance Corporal Dawson and Pfc. Donnelly.

SAM. Downey.

KAFFEE. Downey.

JO. I don't want to talk to you anymore.

KAFFEE. No. I can't accept that. We braved extraordinary elements to get over here. My car ran out of gas halfway up 8th Street. Sam had to walk a quarter of a mile to get help. *(Crosses to Sam and puts an arm around Sam's shoulder.)* Anyway, the wife and I were thinkin' about maybe going into court tomorrow and saving our client's lives, maybe stickin' some homicidal maniacs

behind bars to boot. We thought you might wanna come
along. What do you say?

JO. (*Pause.*) I can't seem to defend people.

KAFFEE. I'm sorry you feel that way. You're my hero,
Joanne. From the first day. You were a lawyer. (*Pause.*)
Live with that.

(*LIGHTS up on courtroom.*)

SERGEANT AT ARMS. Ten-hut.

JUDGE RANDOLPH. Is the defense ready?

KAFFEE. Defense calls Lt. Colonel Roy Jessep.

SERGEANT AT ARMS. Colonel Nathan R. Jessep
will take the stand.

ROSS. Colonel, have you been previously sworn, sir?

JESSEP. No, I have not.

ROSS. (*Holding Bible toward Jessep.*) Sir, would you
raise your right hand and place your left hand on the Bible
please.

(*JESSEP does.*)

ROSS. Do you solemnly swear that the testimony you
will give in this general court-martial will the the truth,
the whole truth, and nothing but the truth, so help you
God?

JESSEP. Yes I do.

ROSS. Would you state your full name, rank and
current billet for the record, please, sir.

JESSEP. Lt. Colonel Nathan Roy Jessep, Barracks CO,
Marine Ground Forces, NAVBASE Guantanamo Bay,
Cuba.

ROSS. Thank you, Colonel. You may have a seat if
you like.

JESSEP. Thank you, Lieutenant.

(JESSEP sits. ROSS crosses to his table and sits; KAFFEE stands.)

KAFFEE. The defense failed to get a deposition from you, so I'm gonna break the cardinal rule and ask you questions without knowing the answers.

JESSEP. Seems a little more sporting that way, Lieutenant.

KAFFEE. Indeed. When you learned of Santiago's letter, did you ask Lt. Kendrick to have a meeting with the members of Second Platoon?

JESSEP. Yes.

KAFFEE. Why?

JESSEP. I felt that Santiago's life might be in danger once word of the letter got out. I had Kendrick tell his men that they were not to take matters into their own hands.

KAFFEE. At the time of this meeting, who was your second in command?

JESSEP. The Company Commander. Captain Matthew Markinson.

KAFFEE. And at present, Captain Markinson is dead, is that right?

ROSS. Objection. I'd like to know just what defense counsel is implying.

KAFFEE. I'm implying simply that at present, Captain Markinson is not alive.

ROSS. Surely Lt. Kaffee doesn't need the Colonel to appear in this court to confirm that information.

KAFFEE. I just wasn't sure if the Colonel was aware that last week Captain Markinson took his own life with a .45 calibre pistol.

JESSEP. I'm aware.

JUDGE RANDOLPH. The witness is aware. The members are aware. We thank you for bringing this to our attention. Lieutenant, please move on.

(*ROSS sits.*)

KAFFEE. Yes, sir. Colonel, at the time of this meeting, when you told Lt. Kendrick to tell his men that they were not to take matters into their own hands, you gave Captain Markinson an instruction as well, is that right?

JESSEP. Indeed. I told Captain Markinson that I wanted the boy transferred off the base immediately.

KAFFEE. You felt Santiago was in danger.

JESSEP. Yes.

KAFFEE. Grave danger?

JESSEP. Is there any other kind?

KAFFEE. When did you learn of Santiago's letter?

JESSEP. Thursday, 7 July.

KAFFEE. What time of day?

JESSEP. In the area of ten hundred.

KAFFEE. 7 July, ten hundred. That's when you told Lt. Kendrick and Captain Markinson that Santiago's life was in grave danger and that the Captain was to transfer him off the base immediately.

JESSEP. Son, is it me, or are we going around in a circle here?

KAFFEE. (*Picks up copy of a transfer from the table.*) I have a copy of the transfer order here. It says that Santiago was scheduled to be moved out at oh two hundred the next morning. Sixteen hours later. Why did Markinson wait 16 hours? Why did Markinson keep a man in danger for 16 hours? (*Puts the transfer order down on the table.*)

JESSEP. There was no transportation off the base until oh two hundred. The oh two hundred was the first flight off. Are these really the questions I've been called here to answer?

KAFFEE. I'm just trying to determine if it's possible that your instructions to the officers weren't carried out.

JESSEP. (*Pause.*) Have you ever served in an infantry unit, son?

KAFFEE. No, sir.

JESSEP. Have you ever served in a forward area?

KAFFEE. No, sir.

JESSEP. Have you ever put your life in another man's hands, ask him to put his life in your hands?

KAFFEE. No, sir.

JESSEP. We follow orders, son. We follow orders or people die. It's that simple.

KAFFEE. Even if that order is illegal?

ROSS. Object.

JUDGE RANDOLPH. Sustained.

KAFFEE. Withdrawn.

JESSEP. Boy, I'd love to know what in the world qualifies you to pass judgment on us.

KAFFEE. Please, sir, I'm not here to pass judgment. The members of the jury are. And they're entitled to the truth.

JESSEP. Is that right?

KAFFEE. Do you disagree?

JESSEP. Certainly not in principle. I disagree only inasmuch as I disagree that a paraplegic is entitled to foxtrot. It'd be nice, it just isn't possible.

KAFFEE. Are you saying it's not possible for this court to hear the truth?

JESSEP. This court? I don't know what that means. I'm saying it's not possible for you to hear the truth.

KAFFEE. Why not, sir?

ROSS. Your Honor, is this dialogue relevant to anything in particular?

KAFFEE. The defendants' commanding officer has just testified that the truth is an unattainable goal. I'd like to know why.

JUDGE RANDOLPH. Colonel, you're under no obligation to address this question.

JESSEP. Captain, for the past month, this man has attempted to put the Marine Corps on trial. I think somebody sure as hell better address this question or people are liable to start listening to him.

KAFFEE. Why is it impossible—?

JESSEP. Because you can't handle it, son. You can't handle the truth. You can't handle the sad but historic reality.

KAFFEE. What reality are you referring to, Colonel?

JESSEP. We live in a world that has walls. And those walls have to be guarded by men with guns. Who's gonna do it? You? (*To Sam.*) You, Lt. Weinberg? I have a greater responsibility than you can possibly fathom. You weep for Santiago, and you curse the Marines. You have that luxury. The luxury of the blind. The luxury of not knowing what I know: That Santiago's death, while tragic, probably saved lives. And my existence, while grotesque and incomprehensible to you ... saves lives. You can't handle it. Because deep down, in places you don't talk about, you *want* me on that wall. You need me there. We use words like honor, code, loyalty. We use these words as a backbone to a life spent defending something. You use them as a punchline. I have neither the time nor the inclination to explain myself to a man who rises and sleeps under the blanket of the very freedom I provide, then questions the manner in which I provide it. I'd prefer you just said thank you and went on your way. Otherwise, I'd suggest you pick up a weapon and stand a post. Either way. I don't give a damn what you think you're entitled to.

KAFFEE. Well, that's what I get for asking questions without knowing the answers. (*Crosses to the defense table.*)

JUDGE RANDOLPH. Colonel Jessep, the court appreciates your time.

JESSEP. (*Stands.*) No trouble, Captain. I love Washington. (*Crosses toward Kaffee.*) Danny, don't look so glum. What is it you people say? Live to fight another time.

KAFFEE. Excuse me, I didn't ask you to step down.

(*JESSEP stops.*)

JESSEP. I beg your pardon?

KAFFEE. I'm not through with my examination. I didn't dismiss you. (*Points to the witness chair.*) Sit down.

ROSS. Lieutenant.

JUDGE RANDOLPH. Counsel.

KAFFEE. I'd like the record to show that the witness got up and walked to the door without being told to step down.

JESSEP. Colonel.

KAFFEE. I beg your pardon?

JESSEP. (*To Judge Randolph.*) I'd prefer it if he addressed me as Colonel or sir. I believe I've earned it.

JUDGE RANDOLPH. Defense counsel will address the witness as Colonel or sir.

JESSEP. (*To Judge Randolph.*) What the hell kind of outfit are you running here?

JUDGE RANDOLPH. And the witness will address this court as Judge or your Honor. I'm certain I've earned it. Take your seat, Colonel.

(*JESSEP sits.*

SAM opens his attaché and removes a log book which HE hands to Kaffee.)

KAFFEE. Submit for Defense Exhibit "A." This is the Tower Chief's Log for Naval Air Station, NAVBASE, Guantanamo Bay, Cuba. It lists incoming and outgoing flights for Thursday, July 7th and Friday the 8th of July. *(Opens the log book, crosses to Jessep.)* Is that your signature? *(Pause.)*

JESSEP. That's my signature.

KAFFEE. I draw the court's attention to the fact that between oh six hundred on Thursday the 7th and oh two hundred on Friday the 8th, no passenger-capable flights left the base. *(HE shows the book to Ross.)*

ROSS. Noted.

(KAFFEE crosses to Judge Randolph.)

JUDGE RANDOLPH. Noted.

KAFFEE. *(Leaves the log book on the Judge's table.)* Colonel, at this time, I'd like to tell you that if you'd like a recess to compose your thoughts, or if you'd like to consult with an attorney, we can arrange—

JESSEP. I don't need an attorney.

KAFFEE. Yes, sir.

ROSS. *(Stands.)* Colonel. I think perhaps—

JESSEP. I said I don't need an attorney.

ROSS. Yes, sir. *(Sits.)*

KAFFEE. *(To Jessep.)* Colonel, a moment ago you said that Willy Santiago's death saved lives.

JESSEP. That's right.

KAFFEE. Given that, I wonder if you could tell us, sir: Are the defendants criminals or heroes? *(Pause.)* Colonel Jessep?

JESSEP. *(Pause.)* I don't suppose that's for me to say.

KAFFEE. I'm asking your opinion, sir. As a military expert. Criminals or heroes?

JESSEP. They're warriors.

KAFFEE. Criminals or heroes, sir?

JESSEP. (*Pause.*) They're heroes.

KAFFEE. Then why in God's name did you go to such trouble to cover up what they'd done?

ROSS. (*Stands.*) Object!!

JUDGE RANDOLPH. Counsel!!

KAFFEE. Why did you fix the log book?

ROSS. Objection! That was totally without—

(*JUDGE RANDOLPH overlaps with ROSS.*)

ROSS. What the hell's the matter with you??!! I request that Lt. Kaffee's remarks be stricken from the record, and that the witness be excused with the court's deepest apologies.

JUDGE RANDOLPH. That's it, I've heard enough. The jury is strictly cautioned. Defense counsel has made a reckless and irresponsible accusation, not the least bit grounded in any evidence whatsoever. (*Overlap ends.*) You're instructed to disregard his remarks entirely. Lt. Kaffee consider yourself in contempt of court. Now are you through with this witness?

KAFFEE. (*Gets the GITMO Log Book from Sam.*) No, your Honor. Submit for Defense Exhibit "B." It's the Tower Chief's Log for Andrews Air Force Base for the evening of July 7th. It seems that at 9:26 p.m., 21:26, an AF-40 transport landed at Andrews with 94 empty seats, having taken off at two minutes past six p.m. It's departure point? ... Colonel? ... Naval Air Station, NAVBASE Guantanamo Bay, Cuba. You know that Kendrick ordered the Code Red on Santiago. Because that's what you told Kendrick to do. And Kendrick follows orders. Or people die, isn't that right, Colonel? You ordered the Code Red, and when it went bad, you cut these guys loose. You had Markinson sign a phony transfer order so it'd look like you tried to move Santiago, you forged the log book so it'd look like the oh two hundred was the first flight out,and you told the doctor to say it was poison so it wouldn't look like a Code Red. You trashed the law. But we understand. You're permitted. You have a greater responsibility than we can possibly fathom. You provide us with a blanket of freedom. We live in a world that has walls, and those walls have to be guarded by men with guns, and nothing's gonna stand in your way of doing it. Not Willy Santiago, not Dawson and Downey, not a thousand armies, not the Uniform Code of Military Justice, and not the Constitution of the United States. That's the truth, isn't it Colonel? I can handle it.

JESSEP. (*Says nothing for a long moment.*) I did my job. I'd do it again.

KAFFEE. You ordered the Code Red.

JESSEP. Yes.

KAFFEE. Say it, Colonel.

JESSEP. I ordered the Code Red.

KAFFEE. Say it again, sir.

JESSEP. I ordered the Code Red.

KAFFEE. (*To Ross.*) Jack.

ROSS. Please the court, I suggest that the jury be dismissed and that we move to an immediate Article 39A Session. The witness has rights.

JUDGE RANDOLPH. Absolutely. The Sergeant at Arms will take the members to an ante-room where you'll wait until further instructions.

JESSEP. All right now, what the hell's goin' on? (*To Judge Randolph.*) Captain, what the hell's goin' on? I'm not familiar with Article 39A. I did it, fine, I ordered the

Code Red. (*Starts to leave*.) Now I'm getting on a plane
and going back to my base.

JUDGE RANDOLPH. (*To the MPs*.) Guard the
prisoner.

JESSEP. What?

(*The MPs start toward Jessep tentatively*.)

ROSS. MPs guard the prisoner.

JESSEP. I ordered a Code Red and everybody's goin' to
pieces like a fuckin' ladies auxiliary.

ROSS. Colonel Jessep you have the right to remain
silent. Any statement you do make can be used against you
in a trial by court-martial. (*Overlaps with Jessep*.)

JESSEP. (*Over the reading of the rights*.) Are you
charging me with a crime? You charging me with ... I'm—
Marine—Marine—this is funny, you know that this is—

ROSS. (*Overlapping Jessep*.) ... or other judicial or
administrative proceeding. You have the right to consult
with a lawyer prior to questioning. This lawyer may be a
civilian lawyer retained at no cost to the United States or a
military lawyer appointed to act as your counsel.

JESSEP. (*Overlapping Ross. JESSEP makes a quick
move toward Kaffee, but is grabbed by two MPs who pull
him back and restrain him*.) I'm gonna tear your eyes right
outa your head and piss in your dead skull! You fucked
with the wrong Marine! The wrong Marine!

ROSS. Colonel Jessep, do you understand these rights
as I've just read them to you?

JESSEP. I'll tell you something, my friend. These
fuckin' people have no idea how to defend a nation. I'm
trying to defend the nation. (*To Kaffee*.) All you did here
today was weaken the country. That's all you did, so you
give yourself a pat on the back. You put people in danger.
Sweet dreams, son.

KAFFEE. Don't call me son. I'm a lawyer. And an officer of the United States Navy. And you're under arrest, you son-of-a-bitch. (*To the MPs.*) The witness is excused.

(*BLACKOUT.*)

MARINES. (*Chanting.*)
LIFT YOUR HEAD AND LIFT IT HIGH
Lift your head and lift it high
CORPORAL DAWSON'S PASSIN' BY
Corporal Dawson's passin' by
LEFT RIGHT
Sound off
SING IT LOUD
Do it again
Three Four
Sound off
Right Left
Stand Proud!

(*JUDGE RANDOLPH raps the gavel on "Stand Proud."
The LIGHTS come up on the courtroom.
JUDGE RANDOLPH reads from the Charge/Sentence
cards.*)

JUDGE RANDOLPH. On the charge of Murder in the Second Degree, the members find the defendants Not Guilty. (*Pause.*) On the charge of Conspiracy to Commit Murder, the members find the defendants Not Guilty. (*Pause.*) On the charge of Conduct Unbecoming a United States Marine ... the members find the defendants Guilty as Charged. (*Pause. Reads from the sentence card.*) The defendants are hereby sentenced by this court to time served in the brig up until this point, and are ordered to be

Dishonorably Discharged from the Marine Corp. (*Long Pause*.) This court-martial is adjourned. (*Raps the gavel*.)

SERGEANT AT ARMS. Ten-hut.

(*JUDGE RANDOLPH stands and exits.*)

SERGEANT AT ARMS. Dismissed.

DAWSON. (*Steps toward Kaffee*.) Why?

KAFFEE. Harold, I'm sorry.

DAWSON. Why?

DOWNEY. I don't understand.

JO. (*Crosses to Downey*.) It's not as bad as it seems.

DOWNEY. Colonel Jessep said he ordered the Code Red.

JO. I know, but—

DOWNEY. Colonel Jessep said he ordered the Code Red. What'd we do wrong?

KAFFEE. Listen—

DOWNEY. What'd we do wrong?

SAM. Ask Dawson.

DAWSON. We did nothing wrong.

SAM. Sure you did.

DOWNEY. Hal?

DAWSON. We did nothing wrong.

SAM. A jury just said your conduct was unbecoming a Marine. What does that mean?

DAWSON. You're the lawyer.

SAM. You're the Marine.

DAWSON. Not anymore.

(*SAM steps toward Dawson*.)

SAM. Corporal? What were you supposed to fight for? (*Pause*.) What were you supposed to fight for?

DAWSON. People who couldn't fight for themselves.

SAM. What were you supposed to fight for?

DAWSON. Willy Santiago. (*Pause.*) We were supposed to fight for Willy.

SAM. No more questions.

SERGEANT AT ARMS. (*Pause.*) Kaffee, I gotta take these guys down to personnel for some paperwork. Gentlemen.

(*Pause. KAFFEE nods to the Sgt. at Arms. DAWSON and DOWNEY start to leave and are almost gone when—*)

KAFFEE. Harold:

(*DAWSON, DOWNEY and SGT AT ARMS stop and turn toward Kaffee.*)

DAWSON. Sir!

KAFFEE. You don't need to wear a patch on your arm to have honor. (*Pause.*)

DAWSON. Ten-hut. (*Pause.*) There's an officer on deck.

(*DAWSON and DOWNEY snap to attention and hold a salute to Kaffee.*
KAFFEE returns a crisp salute.)

DAWSON. Sir. Permission to be dismissed.

KAFFEE. You're dismissed.

(*SGT AT ARMS leads DAWSON and DOWNEY off.*)

ROSS. I didn't know about the Tower Chief's Log.

KAFFEE. The people had a case, Jack.

(*ROSS exits.*)

JO. (*Looks at Kaffee and at Sam, who seem to be in an odd little world.*) You know you two really oughta learn to relax a little. (*Pause. Stands.*) How's 'bout a celebration. I'm buying. Sam? Champagne? Yoo-Hoo?

SAM. Maybe later. I'm gonna go home and talk with my daughter. I think she's gotta be bilingual by now. (*Exits.*)

JO. So what's next for you?

KAFFEE. Staff Sergeant Hector Baines. He went to the movies on company time. What about you?

JO. Me? Oh, you know the usual.

KAFFEE. Just pretty much generally annoying people.

JO. Yeah. (*Pause. Crosses to Kaffee.*) Listen ... are you happy right now? 'Cause you have every reason to be happy right now.

KAFFEE. I am happy. It was very nice of you to ask.

JO. So how 'bout it? You wanna have a drink?

KAFFEE. I'll hook up with you later. I'm gonna get started on Hector Baines. Stand my post for a while.

JO. (*Pause.*) You are, like, seven of the strangest men I've ever met. (*SHE exits.*)

KAFFEE. (*Stands still for a moment, surveys the room picks up his briefcase and begins to leave, singing as he does.*)
LIFT YOUR HEAD AND LIFT IT HIGH
DANIEL KAFFEE'S PASSIN' BY

(*KAFFEE exits as THE SENTRY shifts his rifle. BLACKOUT.*)

End of Play

Other Publications for Your Interest

THE CAINE MUTINY COURT-MARTIAL

(ALL GROUPS—DRAMA)

By HERMAN WOUK

19 men (6 nonspeaking)—Curtained set, desks, chairs and dark blue uniforms of the U.S. Navy.

"The Caine Mutiny," the Pulitzer Prize novel hailed by critics as "the best sea story" and "the best World War II novel," has been adapted by the author in a version which is superior to the novel "in the artfullness of its craftsmanship." (N.Y. Herald Tribune.) "Enormously exciting. It is the modern stage at its best," said the Daily News. "Magnificent theatre," said the Mirror and the Journal-American. It is the court-martial proceedings against a young upright lieutenant who relieved his captain of command in the midst of a harrowing typhoon on the grounds that the captain was psychopathic in the crisis, and was directing the ship and its crew to its destruction. The odds and naval tradition are against the lieutenant. But as the witnesses and experts, some serious, some unwittingly comic, cross the scene of the trial, the weakness in the character of the captain is slowly revealed in a devastating picture of disintegration. An ideal play for all groups.

MEDAL OF HONOR RAG

(LITTLE THEATRE—DRAMA)

By TOM COLE

3 men (2 white, 1 black)

In an army hospital two very dissimilar men confront one another in a verbal sparring match. One, a psychiatrist—the other, "D.J.", a black ex-serviceman and holder of the Congressional Medal of Honor; an "honor" of that hangs on him like an ironic albatross. They also share one common experience—and guilt—they are both survivors in which many others perished. The psychiatrist gradually draws out of D.J. all the guilt, horror and disgust which left him traumatized. Always on guard against "whitie" and his values, D.J. is gradually revealed as a sensitive, intelligent, man nearly destroyed by his Viet Nam experience. His barriers crumbling, D.J. turns on the psychiatrist, exposing the man behind the professional facade. Yet D.J. desperately hopes—and the psychiatrist believes—he can be helped. But before another interview takes place, D.J. goes AWOL—and to get money for unpaid bills—is killed in an attempted robbery. "Cole has handled explosive with great intelligence and rich human understanding . . . beautifully written . . ."—WWD.